BECAUSE I CAN
REMEMBER

BECAUSE I CAN REMEMBER

VOLHA ZHAMOITSINA

To all the seekers of truth and spiritual wisdom, may you find solace, inspiration, and transformation within these pages, and may your journey be filled with love, light, and profound awareness.

May the revelations of my past lives and reincarnations inspire you to explore the depths of your soul and awaken to the eternal truths that reside within.

May you remember the eternal essence of your being and the sacred interconnectedness of all life.

May you awaken to the truth of your divine nature and embrace the beauty and wonder of existence.

With love and blessings,

Volha Zhamoitsina

Contents

Introduction

Welcome to the realm where time is an illusion and the soul's journey transcends the boundaries of lifetimes. "Because I Can Remember" invites you to explore the mysteries of past lives, reincarnation, and spiritual growth deeply. In this captivating exploration, we weave together the themes of expanded consciousness, connection to the higher self and spiritual realms, and the power of inspiration and faith.

I'd like to welcome you on an unforgettable journey through the tapestry of past lives within the pages of this book. My name is Volha Zhamoitsina, I'm a certified hypnotherapist, past life regression specialist, and quantum healing hypnosis practitioner.

With a curious mind, my exploration of past lives and spiritual realms has led to profound discoveries and experiences that I'd like to share with you. Through this journey of self-discovery and spiritual awakening, I unraveled hidden truths and gained unexpected insights into the essence of our existence.

This book delves into the enigmatic journey of the soul's evolution, drawing upon personal experiences, spiritual encounters, and ancient wisdom. As you immerse yourself in the echoes of eternity and the veil of remembrance, you will discover the intricate threads that connect you to your past selves and the souls encountered throughout the ages. Through learning about my journey, I hope you'll find inspiration to embark on your own path of self-discovery and tap into the wisdom of your previous lives.

Additionally, you can expect to gain the following benefits from exploring the profound themes within this book:

- Expanded Consciousness: By delving into the exploration of past lives and the concept of reincarnation, you can expand your consciousness and gain a deeper understanding of the interconnectedness of all beings.
- Connection to Higher Self and Spiritual Realms: Through the exploration of past lives and spiritual encounters, you may deepen your connection to your higher selves and the spiritual realms, gaining a sense of purpose and alignment with your spiritual journey.
- Inspiration and Hope: By sharing personal spiritual insights, the book offers you a sense of inspiration and hope, showing you that no matter the challenges you face, there is always an opportunity for growth and transformation.

"Because I Can Remember" is not just a book – it is a portal to the infinite possibilities of existence, a key to unlocking the mysteries of the universe, and a beacon of light guiding you toward a higher state of consciousness. Dive into its pages and embark on a journey that will forever change the way you perceive yourself and the world around you.

> *"Claim now the parts of yourself that have been locked away from the pure vibration of love and trust."*
> —Aurelia Louise Jones

1

Understanding Reincarnation

The idea of reincarnation has captivated spiritual seekers for centuries because it offers a belief in the soul's eternal nature and its never-ending cycle of rebirth in different physical forms. The soul can evolve through numerous life experiences and accumulate wisdom through this journey of birth, death, and rebirth.

Those who embrace reincarnation also recognize that our souls carry memories and lessons from past lives, which can manifest as unresolved traumas impacting our current lives. We can break free from outdated patterns and beliefs that hinder our personal growth and transformation by acknowledging and healing these deep-seated wounds from previous incarnations.

Through techniques such as past life regression, quantum healing hypnosis, and Akashic records meditation, individuals can explore their past lives to gain profound insights into their present challenges. By engaging in these practices, we can uncover past life traumas, identify recurring patterns, and address ancient wounds that may be holding us back in our current lives.

These methods provide a transformative way to delve into the mysteries of our past lives and understand how they shape our present experiences. Past life regression allows us to access memories and emotions from past incarnations, offering valuable information for healing and personal growth. Quantum healing hypnosis accesses higher states of consciousness to facilitate deep healing and spiritual awakening. Akashic records meditation connects us to universal knowledge stored in the Akashic records, providing insights into our soul's journey through time and space.

By exploring our past lives through these techniques, we can uncover hidden truths, release old wounds, and let go of limiting beliefs. This inner work can lead to profound healing, personal growth, and a deeper understanding of our soul's purpose. Through these powerful practices, we can transform our lives and create a more fulfilling and empowered existence.

2

My First Encounter with Past Lives

A few years ago, a profound sense of longing and restlessness began to stir within me, like a gentle breeze whispering secrets of a grander purpose waiting to be discovered. It was an intangible pull, an invisible thread weaving through the fabric of my being, guiding me toward an unknown destination beyond the horizon of my everyday existence. The yearning grew more insistent with each passing moment, a magnetic force drawing me closer to the edge of a precipice, where the familiar veil of routine and monotony began to thin, revealing glimpses of a world brimming with untold possibilities and hidden truths. The feeling of incompleteness enveloped me like a cloak, urging me to embark on a journey of self-discovery and exploration as I stood on the threshold of a transformative awakening that promised to unravel the mysteries of my soul and illuminate the path to my true purpose.

I began by reflecting on my past experiences, searching for recurring patterns that resonated with my innermost being. I recalled the moments that had ignited a spark when time seemed to freeze, and I was utterly absorbed in pursuits that held deep meaning for me. Through this process of introspection, I slowly began to unravel the threads that would eventually come together to form the intricate tapestry of my purpose.

I realized my purpose wasn't some grand, elusive concept waiting to be discovered in a single epiphany. Instead, it was a culmination of my unique talents, the impact I wanted to have on the world, and the values I held dear. It was about finding alignment between my innermost desires and the external contributions I could make.

One day, I suddenly wanted to meet with a hypnotist, hoping he could help me figure out my life. I'd been caught up in the real estate world for a while, moving from place to place, but deep down, I knew something wasn't right. It felt like I was missing out on something important – there was a bigger picture I couldn't see.

So, I found myself sitting in the hypnotist's office, feeling a bit nervous but also excited to dig deep and uncover what was going on inside me. His eyes seemed to see right through me, and as we talked, it was like he was unlocking parts of me I didn't even know existed.

It was my first time experiencing hypnosis, and I was clueless about its workings. But my desire to discern my life's purpose was overpowering. I was eager to comprehend why I was brought into this world and what my duties and desires were.

The session with the hypnotist proved to be a truly fascinating and eye-opening experience. As I delved into the depths of my subconscious, I was granted a glimpse into not just one but five to six of my past lives. However, this journey was far from ordinary.

Rather than progressing through each past life linearly and chronologically, I leaped from one existence to another without the usual death transition. It was as if I were flickering through the pages of a book, each chapter revealing a different story from another time.

The hypnotist's attempts to guide me through the significant events of a particular life were met with unexpected resistance from my subconscious. Each time we approached a crucial moment, I would suddenly find myself transported to another life and another time, leaving me confused and disoriented.

The experience was thrilling and puzzling as I struggled to make sense of the fragmented glimpses into my past lives. Each shift brought forth a new set of memories, emotions, and connections, painting a complex tapestry of my soul's journey through time and space. It was a surreal and enlightening exploration of my existence, revealing layers of my being that I had never encountered before.

In one of the vivid glimpses into a past life, I was transported to a tumultuous scene that stirred deep emotions within me. As I peered into the vision, I saw a young girl, no older than 16 or 17, with cascading long hair. She stood amidst a field, her gaze fixed on a horizon filled with turmoil and chaos.

The setting bore a striking resemblance to the French Revolution. The air was thick with tension and the distant sounds of battle echoed through the landscape. The scene unfolded before me, with people engaged in a fierce struggle for freedom and justice, their lives hanging in the balance. The sight of people dying in the name of revolution struck a chord deep within me, stirring a wellspring of emotions I could not contain. Tears streamed down my face uncontrollably as I felt the weight of the tragedy unfolding before me.

At that moment, the boundary between past and present blurred, and I was deeply connected to the girl and the harrowing events playing out around her. The authenticity of the experience was undeniable, as goosebumps pricked my skin and a wave of realization washed over me.

All my doubts and skepticism melted away in the face of this powerful revelation. It was as if my soul had orchestrated this poignant encounter to remind me of the intricate tapestry of lives I had lived before. The vision left an indelible mark on my consciousness, a testament to the enduring legacy of my soul's journey through time and history.

Wisdom From A Scary Drowning Experience

In a different scene, I found myself immersed in a heart-wrenching moment as I observed a weathered fisherman, approximately 65 years old, battling against the relentless embrace of drowning waters. As I fought for survival, grappling with the unforgiving forces of nature, a profound realization dawned upon me: the value of life and the inherent strength within each of us to overcome adversity. The harrowing experience served as a poignant reminder that life is a precious gift worth fighting for, a testament to the resilience of the human spirit in the face of life's darkest challenges.

The sight of the fisherman struggling in the water resonated with me, bringing back vivid recollections of my scary encounter with drowning in my recent past. My sister's quick thinking and bravery rescued me from the clutches of the deep, leaving me with an enduring phobia of deep waters that still lingers to this day.

In another life, a nostalgic memory resurfaced as I was transported back to when I was a carefree little girl. Dressed in a charming floral dress, I could vividly picture myself frolicking in the sun-drenched backyard of a cozy house. The air was filled with the joyful laughter of innocence, and my heart brimmed with pure happiness as I reveled in the simple pleasures of childhood. Each moment was a precious gem, sparkling with the magic of carefree days and boundless imagination.

In a different lifetime, I found myself reborn as a solitary rock, a quiet observer in a desolate landscape. The unfamiliar terrain stretched endlessly before me, a vast expanse of emptiness and isolation reverberating with life's haunting absence. Settling into my stony existence, I embraced mindfulness, learning to embrace the present moment amidst the serene silence of my surroundings.

The spacecraft's arrival abruptly upended the quiet balance of my rough life. As the spaceship drew closer, its rounded shape becoming clearer with each passing moment, I watched in awe. The planet was a desolate wasteland, its surface scattered with jagged rocks and boulders.

I had a profound sense that the universe was offering me a glimpse into alternate realities, like the brief preview you get before starting a new chapter or embarking on a new journey. It felt like I was being shown snippets of different past lives, just scratching the surface of their stories without delving deep into any particular experience.

After exploring my past lives, I felt a guiding presence leading me to connect with my guides. I was warmly greeted by an angel, a magnificent being of pure light and ethereal beauty. Their presence radiated a sense of peace and divine wisdom, with eyes that sparkled like stars and a gentle smile that seemed to hold the secrets of the universe. Their wings were vast and shimmering, with feathers that glowed in hues of gold, silver, and iridescent blue. The angel's form seemed to shift and shimmer as if it were made of pure energy and light. Their aura exuded a sense of love and compassion, enveloping me in a warm embrace that felt like coming home. In their presence, I felt a deep sense of connection to the divine and a profound sense of awe and wonder.

The angel then turned around, signifying our journey toward the spiritual guides. The path ahead of us was glowing softly, almost like it had a magical light guiding us toward the spiritual guides we were about to meet. There was a feeling of excitement and reverence in the air as I got ready to connect with these beings who were going to help me on my journey of spiritual growth and enlightenment.

The hypnotist asked about whether the angel had a message for me. However, the angel remained silent. We were about to proceed further when suddenly, the hypnotist began to bring me out of the trance. We were running out of time. It left me without the answer I had been seeking. At that particular moment, I couldn't help but think I could have approached the situation better. The primary question remained unanswered despite leaving the session with a sense of happiness. At that moment, I continued to linger in my thoughts.

Delving into the idea of past lives was a truly enlightening experience for me, a concept that had previously been under my radar. It opened up a new realm of possibilities and perspectives that I had never considered before. I was fascinated by the idea that our souls might have had countless lifetimes, each with its own tale and lessons to be learned. It was like uncovering a treasure trove of knowledge and self-discovery, prompting me to delve deeper into the mysteries of existence and the interconnectedness of our past, present, and future selves.

I stumbled upon the College of Hypnotherapy in Los Angeles a few months later. Without hesitation, I signed up for their one-year course covering past life regression—the main reason I joined. Throughout the year, I immersed myself in the intricate workings of the subconscious mind and its profound capabilities. It was a journey filled with revelation and enlightenment as I delved into the realm of hypnotherapy, uncovering its potential to aid individuals in navigating myriad challenges. From tackling anxiety, phobias, stress, and trauma to breaking free from detrimental habits, boosting self-esteem, and achieving personal aspirations, I witnessed first-hand the transformative power of harnessing the subconscious mind. Through my exploration and practice of hypnotherapy, I gained a deeper understanding of the mind-body connection and discovered the immense capacity for growth and healing within each of us.

An Unexpected Visit From Dolores

I also began to delve into meditation, a practice I had previously dismissed as a waste of time and nonsensical. I began experimenting with self-hypnosis and, much to my astonishment, started unveiling various layers about myself. I derived great satisfaction from regression and managed to uncover multiple past lives.

During one of the deeply meditative sessions, I was graced with the presence of Dolores Cannon in a vision. Her ethereal essence shimmered with wisdom and compassion, enveloping me in a sense of profound peace and enlightenment. As I gazed upon her luminous form, I felt a surge of spiritual energy and a profound connection to the higher realms.

Dolores Cannon, a renowned hypnotherapist and metaphysical teacher, is known for her groundbreaking work in the fields of past life regression and metaphysics. She helped countless individuals explore their past lives, access higher dimensions, and heal deep-seated traumas.

Her presence was palpable, and her message resonated deeply within my soul. She told me that my current exploration of hypnosis was merely scratching the surface of my potential journey. She spoke of a path that would ultimately lead me to Quantum Healing Hypnosis, a method that delves into the realms of past lives, alternate dimensions, and profound healing on a quantum level. Her words were like a guiding light, illuminating the path ahead and instilling me with a sense of purpose and destiny. It was a moment of profound clarity and revelation, igniting a spark within me to continue on this life-changing path of healing and self-discovery.

Upon graduating from hypnotherapy college, I understood the true importance of my very first past life regression session. This experience revealed the answer to my life's purpose indeed, guiding me toward a career in hypnotherapy, past life regression, and quantum healing hypnosis. At that time, my mindset was not open to fully accepting and comprehending the message. However, as I evolved and my consciousness expanded, I could understand it clearly.

So began my journey of self-exploration. This journey was filled with discoveries, unexpected disappointments, and delightful surprises. I learned about the people in my life, and that those I met seemingly 'by chance' actually weren't random encounters at all. They held significance in my past lives.

3

The Neighbors and My Past Life in Japan

When destiny led me to the West Coast of Florida, I discovered a paradise like no other. The exquisite beaches, adorned with white sand and embraced by blue waters, exuded a magical allure. This perfect setting was the ideal place to rejuvenate and find peace. Here, I delved into my first past life regression, a transformative experience that heralded the dawn of a new chapter in my journey. I felt a sense of deep connection to this place. I knew that it was not just a destination but a soulful sanctuary where I could truly connect with my inner self. The experience was a catalyst for growth and self-discovery, igniting a passion to explore the depths of my past lives and uncover the mysteries of my soul.

Surrounded by the beauty of nature, I felt a sense of isolation from the bustling world around me. It was a time when I needed to be alone, away from the noise and distractions of everyday life. Although my friends were not by my side, I found solace in connecting with my neighbors.

There was a single father and his young daughter who lived just a block away. Often, I would take my dog to the park, where he would also bring his own dog and his little girl. She was a charming child between the ages of two and three who quickly stole my heart with her hugs, kisses, and playful nature.

Despite my usual calm demeanor around children, this little girl had a way of drawing me in. We formed a special bond from the moment we met, spending time together at the park and going for walks. She became a bright spot in my day, a companion who brought joy and warmth to my isolated moments.

Initially, I believed that the strong attachment I felt to the girl was due to a deep-seated maternal instinct within me. At my age, the desire to have children of my own was prevalent, and I thought this longing was manifesting in my bond with her. However, as time passed, I realized that the connection we shared went beyond mere maternal instincts.

It was unusual for me to feel such a strong bond with a child who was not my own. I found myself instinctively wanting to protect her from any harm, both consciously and subconsciously. Her presence awakened dormant feelings of motherhood within me, but it was more than just a desire to nurture. Our connection transcended biological ties, touching a part of my soul that I didn't know existed.

Family of Three

While studying hypnotherapy, I delved into the exploration of past lives in search of answers to my current situation and purpose. With past life regression, you have the ability to focus your attention and explore previous lives that resonate with your current desires. For instance, if you're struggling with financial issues in your present life, you can set an intention to revisit a past life where you experienced wealth and abundance. By revisiting that time, you can understand what led to your success and incorporate those feelings and emotions into your current life. Similarly, my intention was to revisit a past life where I was part of a happy, loving family with children.

Through self-guided regression, I ventured into a past life where I experienced the bliss of marriage and parenthood in Japan. In this vivid journey, I saw my happy family of three living in a simple bamboo house. It was poorly constructed, and you could see through the holes in the wall. Our son's bed was built into the wall in the kitchen, right next to the dining table.

I saw myself with my husband and our son, eating a meal for dinner. My spouse approached me, gave me a hug and kissed me. It was such a warm, loving gesture, and I really enjoyed the family time. We were not rich, but we were very happy together as a little family of three.

Another scene unfolded where I was watching my son play in the water outside, his laughter echoing through the air, filled me with joy and energy. As a mother, I patiently watched over him, waiting for him to finish his aquatic adventures. When he was finished swimming, we would walk back home hand in hand, happy and laughing. As I looked at him holding my hand, it struck me how similar he was to the little girl I used to hold hands with in the park. It was as if they were the same soul in different bodies, their eyes twinkling with the same light and their smiles equally charming.

In a stroke of luck, I unexpectedly crossed paths with my previous life's partner on the West Coast of Florida as well. Our short reunion served as a poignant reminder of the interconnected nature of our lives and how history has a way of repeating itself in enigmatic ways. Even though time and distance had kept us apart, reuniting felt like we had never been separated. Our conversations flowed naturally as if we were just continuing from where we left off. It was both sweet and sad, reminding us of the love we once had and the different paths we chose to follow.

The fact that both individuals' names were so similar in this incarnation intrigued me the most. Could it be a sign of confirmation for me, perhaps?

It is truly fascinating how connections from past lives can manifest in our present reality, even if only for a brief moment. Sometimes, we meet people and feel an inexplicable connection, unaware that we shared a history in a previous existence. Our physical forms may change, but the essence of our souls remains constant, bridging the gap between the past, present, and future.

4

Regression to the 18th Century

I was embarking on my training in past life regression with an open mind and no specific expectations. Approaching this practice with curiosity, openness, and receptivity, I created the space for profound experiences and insights to unfold naturally. I understood that past life regression can be a deeply transformative and enlightening process. By letting go of preconceived notions and allowing myself to be guided by the process, I opened myself up to uncovering hidden truths, healing past traumas, and gaining valuable insights into my soul's journey across lifetimes. Thus, the expedition to one of my previous existences started. I developed a resolution to relive a past life where I was prosperous, filled with joy, and content.

And a time travel journey began...

The first thing that caught my attention was my bedroom. I observed the drapes, curtains, carpet, and an abundance of heavy fabric adorning every corner—the upholstered furniture with floral patterns. The floral patterns seemed to be everywhere. The room exuded an 18th-century style with its massive furniture and huge windows, giving it a grand and imposing presence. My initial reaction was, "Wow, this place desperately needs some updates and remodeling."

The room felt elegant for that time but out of sync with my current minimalist inclinations and obsession with orderliness. Initially, it was overwhelming, but soon I found it amusing. Then, amidst this peculiar setting, I spotted a familiar face from my current life—a friend with whom I had once shared a romantic relationship in this present life. It was an intimate scene in my bedroom, flirting and laughing. He was dressed in the attire of the 18th century, acting as if he were some kind of lord or ruler. It felt like my friend just put on the wig to play a role game. As our eyes met, laughter erupted from within me. It was a sight to behold—witnessing someone I knew so well in such a hilarious and vastly different situation in an entirely different era.

Naturally, my first reaction to his outfit was, "What on earth are you wearing?" I found myself dressed in an extravagant, voluminous gown with layers upon layers of underskirts, giving it a fluffy and grandiose appearance. The scene before me radiated with romance. He was my lover in that lifetime, too. It was a love filled with playfulness, flirtation, and a sense of lightheartedness and belonging. I felt loved.

However, It did not carry the weight of a boyfriend or a husband, and I felt more independent. It was as if we were engaged in a purposeful game, and I willingly played along, embracing the enchanting experience.

The scene then shifted to my deathbed, the last day of my life. I had a high fever, and many servants were looking after me. They were applying cold compresses to my forehead; they'd dampen a bandage or towel, place it on my forehead, and replace it with a fresh, cool one once it warmed. Most of the servants were men.

In that regression, I didn't draw any conclusions about our identities. I found the entire spectacle highly entertaining. I realized it was set around the 18th century, but, as I already mentioned, I didn't attempt to identify us by names or establish any historical links. I simply had a great time and thoroughly enjoyed this regression. It was a fun experience, and I just let it be. After a while, I put it out of my mind. It was just another experience that I ticked off my list and then forgot about for some time.

5

Madame de Pompadour and the King

Several months had passed before I found myself back in the sprawling city of Los Angeles. After spending some time exploring other states, my return remained a well-kept secret. Unexpectedly, a text message from my friend, whom I saw in my past life regression as my lover and I described earlier, broke the silence. I couldn't understand how he could have known about my presence in LA. His inquiry cut straight to the point, asking if I was indeed in town.

The arrival of this text message and the sudden reappearance of this individual stirred up memories of a past life regression I had undergone several months ago. Something about the situation triggered a deep intuition within me as if there were still hidden truths and undiscovered information waiting to be unveiled. It strongly felt like there was more to that regression than I had initially realized, and a sense of urgency convinced me to explore further and unearth the hidden depths within.

As I thought about the integration, the memory came rushing back. I could clearly remember that moment of regression, and it got me thinking. If I had many servants in the past, it must mean I was an important person in those times. It made me curious to find out more, so I looked into French history in the 18th century. I found a resemblance to the king, which gave me goosebumps. It felt like nothing had changed. In my regression, I saw him, and that led me to search for his lover. I was amazed to discover Madame de Pompadour.

The romance between Madame de Pompadour and Louis XV was a captivating tale that unfolded amidst the opulent and extravagant court of Versailles. Madame de Pompadour, born Jeanne-Antoinette Poisson, was a woman of exceptional beauty, intelligence, and charm. As the official chief mistress of King Louis XV, she became one of the most influential and powerful figures of her time.

As I was browsing pictures from that era, the lavish drapes, abundant fabrics, and expansive rooms served as constant reminders of my past life regression. It was as if I were peering into a mirror reflecting my previous existence. The memories washed over me, sending a tingling sensation down my spine. The realization struck me: I had indeed been a person of great significance in that time.

However, my skeptical nature kicked in, and doubts began to cloud my belief. It seemed too fantastical, too unreal, to be true. Maybe it was a mistake or a coincidence. Perhaps there was another explanation. But then, a memory resurfaced, reminding me of the circumstances of my fatality in that past life. As I delved into the search results, I discovered that Madame de Pompadour had indeed passed away from a high fever, exactly how it was in my regression. The realization sent a chill down my spine. It was the very same way I had perished in that previous existence. Slowly but surely, the puzzle pieces were fitting together, leaving me both astounded and filled with a sense of awe.

When I told my friends about this news, I received skepticism and strange looks in return. They seemed to think I had lost my mind. Determined to delve deeper into the mystery, I resolved to conduct further investigations on my own.

Karmic Debts Repaid

It had been some time since I last explored this subject, but a strange revelation emerged during my most recent guided meditation. As I delved into the Akashic records, information regarding the couple began to surface, adding another layer of intrigue to the unfolding story.

In my spiritual journey, I have been enlightened about the karmic debts I have cleared from my past lives. It has come to my attention that in my previous existence during the 18th century, I was entangled in a complex dynamic with a man who was married. I was his mistress. However, I made a conscious choice not to repeat the patterns of the past in my current life. I refused to settle for a relationship where I was not prioritized as the number one woman in his current life. I chose to break free from the cycle and prioritize self-love. Through this experience, I have learned a valuable lesson about not settling for anything less than a faithful and devoted partner who sees me as his one and only.

In a fascinating twist of fate, it seems that the king himself also had karmic debts to settle in this lifetime. In his past life, Madame de Pompadour had a daughter from a previous marriage whom he had refused to accept. However, in this current life, he has found himself falling deeply in love and is on the verge of marrying a beautiful woman who has a daughter of her own. Remarkably, he has embraced this child as his own, breaking the cycle of past rejection and clearing the karmic debt from his previous life. It is a beautiful testament to the power of love and growth in our journey towards spiritual enlightenment.

I received a profound message from my spirit guides, revealing that we have finally cleared our karmic debts. We no longer owe anything to each other. However, the significance lies in the fact that we have found comfort in knowing that we have a deep connection that has spanned centuries. I am genuinely grateful that we have reconnected in this lifetime, as it signifies the completion of our lessons and the resolution of our karmic ties.

Indeed, the essence of the soul remains constant throughout lifetimes, regardless of the physical form it inhabits. It is like an unwavering light that accompanies us on our journey through different experiences and embodiments. While the external appearance may change, the core of who we are—the essence that radiates within us—remains unaltered.

This eternal aspect of our being allows for the exploration of various roles, identities, and expressions throughout different lifetimes. It is a beautiful reminder that our true nature transcends the limitations of the physical and embraces the infinite possibilities of existence.

6

Memories of Paris

Have you ever wondered why you feel a deep resonance with a specific era in history? What captivates you about certain historical films? Have you ever thought about how events from past lives influenced your current hobbies, including the books, movies, and media you enjoy reading and watching? We often attribute our affinity for certain creations and periods to our ancestors, but could it be possible that we are one of those ancestors?

In the past, I never entertained such thoughts. My mind-set was too limited to consider such possibilities. However, with a broader perspective and an open mind, I now find myself contemplating these ideas. While there are some souls experiencing life on Earth for the first time, there are also many who have been reincarnating throughout the ages, witnessing the evolution of our planet. And I am one of those souls.

I have come to realize that I may have been a part of the very history that captivates me. It's a fascinating thought to consider that the era I feel drawn to and the stories I immerse myself in could be a reflection of my own past experiences. Perhaps I have witnessed the rise and fall of civilizations and the triumphs and struggles of humanity throughout the ages. This idea allows me to connect with and understand the world around me on a whole new level. It reminds me that I am not just a passive observer of history but an active participant in its unfolding.

During my time at a fashion school in Hamburg, Germany, I vividly recall immersing myself in the captivating study of costume history. Our focus was on the enchanting world of Rococo fashion history, a subject that truly held me spellbound. I can still hear myself gleefully uttering its name repeatedly as if each syllable brought me joy and delight. Little did I know then that this fascination was not merely a passing interest but a connection to my past. I was studying Rococo fashion with a passion, and I had been involved in it without realizing it at the time. This seductive style, which drew inspiration from figures like Madame de Pompadour and Louis XV, was intricately woven throughout my previous incarnations. Reflecting on this realization, I find it fascinating how we are often drawn back to the places that once held our hearts and were unequivocally called home.

During my time as a fashion design student and intern at a renowned designer's atelier in Hamburg, an incredible opportunity presented itself: an invitation to join the backstage preparations during Paris Fashion Week at the Carrousel du Louvre. The mere thought of it set my heart racing with excitement. With a mix of nerves and anticipation, I gathered my belongings and set out to the fashion capital of the world.

As soon as I landed in Paris, I could feel the electric energy in the air. The city was alive with the buzz of creativity and style. As I stepped into the bustling backstage area, an exhilarating whirlwind of activity greeted me. Models, stylists, and makeup artists moved with purpose, bringing the designer's vision to life.

With wide eyes and a determined spirit, I immersed myself in the tasks at hand. Assisting with fittings, ensuring garments were flawlessly displayed, and lending a helping hand wherever needed, I felt an incredible sense of purpose. The atmosphere was charged with anticipation and the pursuit of perfection.

Paris is recognized as a global fashion capital, with its biannual Fashion Week events being of utmost importance in the fashion industry. Twice a year, fashion enthusiasts, designers, models, and industry professionals from around the world flock to Paris to witness the latest trends, designs, and collections from top fashion houses. Paris Fashion Week provides a stage for designers to showcase their creativity and innovation, setting the bar for future fashion seasons. It is an iconic event that not only influences the fashion landscape but also shapes the global fashion industry as a whole.

After the exhilaration of Paris Fashion Week, I had the opportunity to explore the enchanting city on my own terms. With the bustling energy of the fashion world behind me, I set out to experience the true essence of Paris. The day was mine to savor, to immerse myself in the vibrant vibrations that permeated every corner of the city.

I started my journey at the famous Eiffel Tower, a symbol of Paris's magical charm. Stepping onto its grounds, I was instantly overcome with a mix of excitement and wonder. The iron lattice structure soared above me, reaching toward the heavens as if inviting me to explore its secrets. The intricate architectural details, meticulously designed and crafted, spoke volumes about the city's rich history and artistic prowess. As I gazed up at the towering monument, I couldn't help but appreciate the sheer magnitude of human ingenuity that went into its creation. It stood as a testament to the human capability of turning dreams into reality, and I felt a surge of inspiration course through my veins.

When I reached the observation deck, the breathtaking panorama of Paris stretched out before me. Famous sites in the city, such as the Louvre and Notre Dame Cathedral, were visible in the distance, adding to the allure and charm of the scene. At that moment, I realized that Paris truly lived up to its reputation as the "City of Love" and the epitome of romance. The charm and allure were not merely clichés but a tangible essence that enveloped me, leaving an indelible mark on my soul.

With a grateful heart, I bid farewell to the Eiffel Tower, knowing its magic would forever remain etched in my memories. As I continued my journey through the enchanting streets of Paris, I carried with me a newfound appreciation for the city's beauty, history, and unique energy that made it truly one of a kind.

My visit to the Palace of Versailles, though, was what really lit a fire under me. I felt a wave of liberation sweep over me with every step I took toward the palace, relieving me of the burdens of daily life and enabling me to enjoy the moment fully.

Here I was, enveloped by the vibrations of history, sensing a strange connection to the past. I came to understand that this location had more meaning for me. It was more than simply a tourist destination; it was a place where my soul found comfort and resonance. It felt like my own energy and the energy of the past combined to create a potent synergy that spoke to my soul. Upon reflection now, I realized that my trip to the Palace of Versailles was more than just a visit —it was a return home. It was the reunion of a part of myself that had been quietly awaiting acknowledgment.

7

The Image of Elizabeth I: Reality or Illusion?

One day, while enjoying my coffee and relaxing on the couch, something strange happened. After finishing my coffee, I looked at the bottom of the cup and saw an image. It was a woman's profile; every feature was angled perfectly—her forehead, her chin, her nose—it was like a portrait in profile. I asked myself if it was me, and it felt like the answer was yes. The thought also crossed my mind that it was a queen.

I couldn't believe what I was daydreaming. A queen? Me? I chuckled to myself, thinking it was just my imagination playing tricks on me. But as I stared at the intricate details of the picture, I couldn't help but feel a sense of curiosity. Who was this queen?

Excited beyond my control, I hurriedly snatched my phone and began searching for images of any queens. As

I compared the portraits in my coffee cup to the ones on the internet, I couldn't help but notice the striking similarities. Everything matched perfectly with the high forehead, pointed chin, and nose. I sat there, staring at the image in disbelief. How could this be? Queen Elizabeth I, one of the most influential and iconic queens in history, appears in the remnants of my morning coffee. It felt surreal.

The "Virgin Queen" of England, Elizabeth I, was the daughter of Anne Boleyn and King Henry VIII. She reigned from 1558 until she died in 1603. Strong leadership, victorious military campaigns, and the thriving arts and culture during Queen Elizabeth I's reign are among the things that people remember about her. She was a significant figure in English history.

She was known for her intelligence, determination, and strength. She defied societal norms and expectations, ruling with an iron fist and leaving a lasting impact on England and the world.

As time went on, I found myself battling with the idea that I might have once been a queen in a past life. The concept felt foreign and unsettling, stirring up fears of what accepting such a revelation could mean for my present reality.

8

Paying Off Karma: From Queen to Maid

Months passed without much thought given to the idea until unexpected triggers reignited those buried emotions. It was as if the universe was nudging me to explore this uncharted territory, urging me to confront the uncomfortable truths that lay dormant within me. With each passing day, the pull towards unraveling the mysteries of my past life as a queen grew stronger, beckoning me to delve into the depths of my soul.

One particular moment from my early 20s came to mind: immediately after graduating from a Belarusian high school, I decided to work as an au pair in Germany, to travel overseas to live with a host family and give childcare services in return for housing, food, and a meager stipend. The French word "au pair" means "on a par" or "equal to," which captures the idea that the au pair is not an employee but rather a member of the family. Au pairs typically assist with child-care responsibilities including watching and playing with kids, participating in homework, and occasionally helping with little tasks at home that are connected to the kids. The main focus is cultural exchange, language learning, and building a relationship with the host family.

With only one suitcase, 50 Deutschmarks in my pocket, and a one-way ticket for the bus trip, I set off on my journey as an au pair in Germany. It was a leap of faith into the unknown, but I was determined to embrace the adventure and make the most of this opportunity for personal growth and cultural exchange. Despite the limited resources, I was excited about the experiences that awaited me in a new country and with a new host family.

It was a big decision that ended up shaping my life in ways I never could have predicted. Living with a wealthy host family in a beautiful mansion was both exciting and intimidating. But beneath all the luxury, I quickly realized that things weren't as perfect as they seemed. The host mother was cold and distant, and her attitude made me feel like I didn't belong in their world.

Having to wake up very early every morning to ride a bike to the bakery and pick up fresh bread was a real struggle, especially with Hamburg's reputation for cold, rainy weather year-round. It made me wonder why I had chosen this path. Feeling lost and alone in a place so different from what I was accustomed to only added to my uncertainty and apprehension.

There's a moment from my time as an au pair that still lingers painfully in my memory. I vividly recall the host mother casually labeling me as "the maid" in front of her friends during a social gathering. The room fell silent as her words hung in the air, suffocating me with embarrassment and hurt. I felt like an invisible presence in my own skin, reduced to a mere servant in their eyes. It was a stark awakening to my standing in their household, leaving me grappling with a profound sense of worthlessness and disillusionment.

But things started to look up when I moved on to a new host family. This was a fresh start for me, a chance to chase my dream of studying fashion design and working various jobs to support myself. It was a time filled with hope and possibility – a chance for me to carve out my own path. My new host family was absolutely supportive of my decision to pursue further studies.

Looking back on those challenging times, I see them as lessons that shaped me. The experience of being undervalued and mistreated taught me to appreciate my worth and to keep pushing forward. Life is full of ups and downs, and it's a journey of growth and self-discovery.

In one life, you reign as a queen; in another, you serve as a maid. Positions reversed.

9

A Glimpse into the Past

Time passed, and I would sometimes allow myself to ponder the possibilities of that past life as Elizabeth, and it would linger with me. This went on for around a year since I first saw the portrayal of the queen in my coffee cup. Sometimes, I would try to push the thoughts away and dismiss the idea, but on other occasions, I would consider that perhaps there was a reason why all this information kept coming back to me. It was as if the universe was giving me little clues, allowing me some time to digest the information, and then presenting me with more. Eventually, I began to entertain the thought that maybe there was a past life involved, or perhaps it was just an imprint. But if it was an imprint, what could be the reason for me to see it?

What is an imprint?

"They can withdraw information from the Akashic records and imprint this information into their soul, and it will then be their experience... If one were to come to this planet from another planet or dimension without the aid of imprints, one would be totally lost. One would not understand customs, religions, politics, or how to act in a social environment." – *Dolores Cannon, The Keepers of the Garden.*

Group Past Life Regression Meditation

To learn more about the era of Queen Elizabeth the First, I undertook a past life regression meditation with a group. So, it was a fun setting, and I didn't expect much. It was more about entertaining myself and seeing if I could gather any new information about that time.

As I delved into the past, I could see the scene: a carriage rolling in, with crowds of people loudly cheering on both sides of the road. I was a little girl with long hair and a flowing dress. Despite my resistance, I was taken to the palace. I didn't want to go and refused to walk, but two individuals flanked me on either side, forcing me towards the building.

Fast-forwarding through time, I saw myself as a young woman with her hair let down but clipped back to keep it off her face. This young woman was standing on the second or third floor of a building, looking down at the grounds through the window. A sense of worry was palpable; she was concerned about something. She had responsibilities that she was in charge of.

During this regression, another scene that unfolded before me was a carriage with horses and a large flag returning to what seemed to be a battlefield. The atmosphere was surprisingly joyful.

While I didn't get the significant validation I was seeking, it felt as if the universe offered me a brief snapshot of my past life, as if to say, "Here's a small preview; stay tuned for more."

Despite my initial frustration, I gradually began to understand the universe's cryptic way of communicating.

It wasn't about seeking validation or proving my worth; it was about learning and growing. It was about understanding the different aspects of my soul, the multiple lives it had lived, and the wisdom it had accumulated over the centuries.

The universe was not withholding information from me but was simply guiding me to discover it at my own pace. The brief snapshots of my past life were not meant to provide immediate answers but to stimulate curiosity and self-exploration. This journey was not about the destination but about the process of self-discovery and transformation.

I felt a profound sense of peace as this realization dawned on me. I was no longer desperate for validation or answers. Instead, I was eager to uncover more about my past life, my soul's journey, and the wisdom it had to offer. After all, as the saying goes, one step is the start of a thousand-mile journey. And this was just the beginning of my journey – one that promised to be filled with self-discovery, growth, and a deeper understanding of the universe and myself.

10

The Unveiling of a Bond

On my journey to expand my consciousness, I stumbled upon a captivating book called "Telos- Volume 2" by Aurelia Louise Jones. As I delved into its pages, a wave of enlightenment washed over me, filling my mind with the essence of knowledge and guiding me on my path of evolution. Within the ancient tome, I discovered not just words but profound revelations that resonated deep within my soul, propelling me forward on my quest for spiritual awakening.

I learned that Saint Germain, an Ascended Master, has had many incarnations; there were a few names on the list. "In one of his many previous incarnations he was Joseph, the father of Master Jesus, who lived 2,000 years ago. He also incarnated as the prophet Samuel, Christopher Columbus and Francis Bacon, the true author of the Shakespearian plays."

The name Francis Bacon caught my attention for some reason. I searched the internet for the years he was alive and came across the 16th and 17th centuries, an era of Elizabeth I. Francis Bacon, an influential figure in the 16th century, known for his contributions to philosophy, science, and literature. Born on January 22, 1561, in London, England, Bacon served as Attorney General and Lord Chancellor of England, holding important positions in the government.

Bacon is often regarded as the father of empiricism and the scientific method. He emphasized the importance of observation and experimentation in understanding the natural world, advocating for a more systematic and evidence-based approach to scientific inquiry. Bacon's work laid the foundation for modern scientific thinking, influencing prominent scientists such as Isaac Newton.

In addition to his scientific contributions, Bacon was a prolific writer and philosopher. He is best known for his essays, which cover a wide range of topics, including politics, ethics, and human nature. Bacon's writing style is characterized by its clarity, conciseness, and wit, making his works accessible to a wide audience.

Despite his significant achievements, Bacon's career was marred by controversy. In 1621, he was charged with corruption and accepting bribes, leading to his dismissal from office and a period of disgrace. Bacon spent his later years focusing on his writing and philosophical pursuits, leaving behind a lasting legacy as one of the most important figures of the 16th century.

However, the most shocking revelation came when I learned from my online research that Queen Elizabeth I had a secret son she gave away to protect her power and throne.

This son turned out to be Francis Bacon, an incarnation of Saint Germain. The revelation blew my mind and added a new layer of intrigue to my quest for enlightenment.

In my newfound awareness of the connection between St. Germain and Queen Elizabeth I, I had moments of doubt, wondering if he truly was her son. Some online sources mentioned her never having a child, casting uncertainty on this relationship. However, my doubts were soon dispelled when I stumbled upon the book "Understanding Twin Flame Union: the Ascension of St. Germain and Portia" by Claire Heartsong and Catherine Ann Clemett. The book clearly states:

"Indeed, my mother was Queen Elizabeth of England who epitomized the colonization of nations, which was part of personal memory of 'star-wars'. Indeed beloveds, it is true –Queen Elizabeth was a grand fiery-haired one, to be sure, with a grand heart and a grand mind and a grand vision and a grand knowingness. She conceived that which be I and she sent me off onto other parentage, the home of the Bacons, where I became quite a boar, as it were."

"So you are confirming that Francis Bacon was the son of Queen Elizabeth, who gave her son to one of the ladies-in-waiting?"

ST. GERMAIN: "Indeed."

Another example is when Portia, his twin flame, speaks about him:

"I watched over him upon the birthing bed when he was delivered in great secrecy–a great shrouding. There were hushed whispers and dimmed lights when the cries of birthing broke forth through the dry lips of the mother with flaming red hair. My heart ached for her and for the sibling who was born. A young maiden, who was a lady-in-waiting and also a wet-nurse, took the wee babe away, at the mother's insistence, before he even had a suckle at her breast."

In this book, I discovered the profound connection between Francis Bacon (Saint Germain) and Queen Elizabeth I, confirming the truth of their bond. In the 16th century, she gave away her son to keep the throne and her power. Today, I would give it all away to have a child. The priorities have changed over the centuries.

The information I was receiving was quite heavy on my heart. It was difficult to digest, and I had to give myself breaks, sometimes for a few days or weeks, before moving forward with the next revelation. Subconsciously, I knew that it might be painful and unpleasant once I started delving into these discoveries. This underlying awareness probably led me to initially reject the idea that it could be my past life because, deep down, I knew that there was more painful information waiting to be uncovered.

In this moment of realization, I made a solemn promise to myself: to let go of all resentment, regrets, guilt, and grudges that had weighed me down. I understood that forgiveness was not an easy task, but it was a necessary one for my spiritual evolution. I knew that by letting go, I could truly embrace the beauty and potential of my present life.

Though life is not always woven with these threads, we frequently wish to see ourselves as happy, prosperous rulers.

It is essential to embrace this truth without judgment. Our souls actively choose the scenarios they wish to experience, be they good or bad. Each experience serves a purpose in our soul's evolution, even if the reasoning eludes us in the present moment. The puzzle will eventually make sense once the pieces start to fit together.

I gained profound insight into why we are born without conscious recollection of our previous lives. The weight of emotions and memories can be utterly overwhelming. That's when I realized how wonderful it is to start over, free from the burdens of the past. And, remarkably, we possess the freedom to choose whether or not we wish to remember. If one finds contentment in not knowing one's past self, that choice is just as valid. We all have a free will.

"We have all been healers and we have all been murderers. It is time to forgive ourselves for all that we have done, and all that has been done in our name."

–Aurelia Louise Jones

11

Past Life with My Father

One day, I chose to engage in Akashic records meditation to seek further insights about my past life. My goal this time was to delve deeper into the life of Queen Elizabeth I and the actual events that transpired.

As soon as I reached a hypnotic state of being able to receive messages, the information began pouring in swiftly. It concerned my father, who grew up without his biological father and was placed in four different foster homes throughout his childhood, where he underwent a horrific and painful phase of his life. My grandma remarried and could not keep him in the family. A few days ago, we were actually talking about his karma and his childhood and why he had to experience it.

So the message in my meditation was that his pain in this existence stemmed from having to go through it himself to learn what it's like to be abandoned and forced to grow up without parents. In a previous life, he was Robert Dudley, the biological father of Elizabeth's son. This child was the secret child of the two and was given to the Bacon family. In this life, my father had to balance his karma in such a way.

At some point, I wanted to halt the influx of these messages. I even protested in my mind that they didn't make any sense. It felt awkward and weird, as it didn't align with my reality. However, I was told that it would begin to make sense once I started putting together all the information that I have gathered in my present life.

It is indeed intriguing to consider the possibility of interconnected relationships across different lifetimes. The concept of soulmates, soul connections, and past-life relationships suggests that the souls we encounter in our current lives may have played different roles in our past lives, such as lovers, family members, friends, or even adversaries. The idea that my father in this life could have been my lover in a previous life adds another layer of complexity to the dynamics of relationships and the eternal journey of the soul. Exploring these spiritual and metaphysical concepts can offer a deeper understanding of the connections we share with others and the lessons we are meant to learn throughout our soul's journey.

The realization triggered a memory buried deep within me—a recollection from a few years ago. I can still vividly recall a time in my early twenties when I was studying fashion in Hamburg, Germany. I decided to visit my parents in Eastern Europe, and my father picked me up from the train station. As I sat in the back seat of the car, I caught a glimpse of him in the rearview mirror. To my surprise, instead of seeing my dad, I saw an unfamiliar older man with a beard and a stern expression. This unexpected sight frightened me to the point where I couldn't bring myself to look directly at my father for the duration of my visit home. It left me with a heavy feeling inside.

I had no clue that there could be prior lives back then. I was sad and perplexed when I left home. Now, though, things are starting to make sense. The timing was perfect for their release as the intense emotions and feelings came to the surface in a wave. I was prepared.

My guides sent me a telepathic message, telling me to relax in a warm salt water bath and let the information really sink in. I was sick to my stomach and had a pounding headache from the weight of everything I had learned and experienced that day during the meditation. It was all too much for my mind to handle.

It took me several days to purge the heavy energy from my system and genuinely liberate myself from the oppressive weight. It was a task I had been evading for some time, and subconsciously, I was aware that it required my attention. Once it was brought to my consciousness and processed, I felt like I had accomplished a considerable amount of work.

I extended my love and compassion from a place devoid of judgment. I offered my forgiveness to those who had wronged me in the past and to myself for holding onto the pain for so long.

This journey wasn't easy; it took time, patience, and a lot of inner strength. But it was worth every moment of discomfort. I learned so much about myself and my ability to heal.

I realized that I have the power to control my emotions and reactions, and I can release any negativity that may be holding me back.

This is my journey, my healing, and my transformation. And I am grateful for every moment of it.

12

Grandma's Visit from the Other Side

One day during Akashic records guided meditation, I saw myself jumping on a trampoline in front of a huge library structure. I was jumping so high as if reaching the cosmos, the galaxy, and the stars. It was so much fun. Then, the guiding voice instructed me to place myself in front of the library door. I thought to myself, "The fun is over," and then I felt somebody pulling my sleeve. When I looked down, I saw a little girl. She asked if she could join me on a trip to the library, and I agreed.

As we entered the library, I had forgotten about her but suddenly felt a strong urge, which confused me, to call upon my grandma, my father's mother. I called out her name, and there she was, dressed in white, walking towards me with a radiant smile. A pure energy of love emanated from her, a stark contrast to the grandma I knew in life. It was undeniably her, with the same voice, the same dress but in white, and the same charisma.

She passed away a few years ago, and I didn't have a chance to say goodbye. Unfortunately, she was not my favorite when she was alive, and her energy was very heavy on me. I tried to avoid her in any way. But it came to my awareness that someone from the other side was trying to communicate with me and had a message for me. I thought that she might want to control me from the other side as well, and I was not really looking forward to it. But one of my spiritual teachers told me that it might have been her role to play while she was alive, and her spirit is no more than pure love.

Tears of joy streamed down my face as I embraced her and apologized for avoiding her and not saying goodbye before she passed. She smiled, completely accepting and devoid of judgment or negativity. It was pure, unconditional love and light that she exuded. And she had a message for me, one about my future, my calling, and especially my future family. She also mentioned that a little girl is constantly pulling her sleeve, asking if it's time for her to go to Earth. The girl has been patiently waiting for her turn, preparing and studying for her incarnation.

I listened intently as she delivered her message. She expressed her pride in me for figuring out how to connect with her on my own and for my curiosity and desire to expand my consciousness. We expressed our love for each other, and then she was gone, leaving me to continue my guided meditation journey alone.

I spent a lot of time reflecting on this experience, and everything started to make sense. I realized that there is no separation, and it is possible to communicate with spirits on the other side. I had learned how to do it. My perspective on death shifted, and I embraced a new understanding. There is no such thing as death; there is only transition.

You Have a Visitor

Time passed, and I completed my college studies in hypnotherapy while finishing my internship for Quantum Healing Hypnosis certification. Both techniques have their benefits, and the choice between the two would depend on the individual's personal goals. I really enjoy engaging in quantum healing hypnosis, as it allows me to connect with a higher power. Even though we often label it as the subconscious for simplicity, the true essence of this energy goes beyond any specific name. In reality, we are working with a collective energy that transcends individual labels.

I had only one client left before becoming a practitioner. As usual, I was practicing energy healing myself and listening to high-frequency music to connect with my higher soul and seek answers about my current situation. Suddenly, a telepathic voice said, "You have a visitor." I was puzzled, wondering who could be visiting me. But tears of joy streamed down my cheeks as I realized it was my grandma. She had come to congratulate me on completing my internship and becoming a quantum healing hypnosis practitioner. She was incredibly proud of me.

At some point, I feared that she had come to tell me that she would be taking my father, as his health was not the best. However, she reassured me that they were not taking anyone over at that time. Instead, she revealed that a soul was waiting to come to Earth, a soul that had been waiting for quite some time. I understood exactly what she meant.

The pressure was intense, especially considering I wasn't even dating anyone at that time. But my grandma continued, assuring me that I would meet my future husband soon. I cried throughout our conversation, overwhelmed with emotions.

As she delivered the message, she paused, and I sensed she didn't want to leave as if it were our last time together. I asked if she needed to go, and she nodded. This time, she lingered as if there was nothing left to discuss or explain. Everything had been said. And then she was gone.

13

An ET-Hacked Session

In addition to conducting hypnotherapy consultations with clients, I occasionally have private mentoring sessions. These sessions are with my more experienced mentors, who sometimes assist me in my personal growth.

Recently, I had a standard, unremarkable online session with one of my mentors. I had arranged for some light, and she set up calming music to play in the background. To enhance my relaxation, I put on my headphones, and the hypnosis session began. Since I had already experienced going into a deep state before, I was able to enter a trance rather quickly. Then the voice in my headphones faded and was replaced by a loud noise that sounded like a scene from a movie if there was a coded message in the noise.

The noise increased, growing progressively louder and unbearable. I opened my eyes and looked at her. She seemed puzzled as to why I had disrupted the session. I tried telling her that I couldn't hear her, but she seemed unable to hear me as well. I unplugged my headphones from my computer, only for the noise to fill the room, echoing off every corner. I repeated, louder this time, "I can't hear you!" but she remained oblivious.

After that, I decided to record the disruptive noise on my phone. The moment I started recording, the noise began to fade, and I was able to hear my mentor again. She was confused, so I tried to explain what had happened and describe the noise. Despite the disruption, we resumed our session. Later, when I received the recording, I fast-forwarded to the part where I stated, "I cannot hear you." To my surprise, the recording only captured the music and my mentor's voice in the background, with no trace of the noise.

Initially, I thought that someone had interfered with my session. The noise sounded like a cryptic message; this was the first suspicion that popped into my mind. I also considered that it would require advanced technology to separate two distinct sounds playing simultaneously.

I decided to send the recording of the disruptive noise from my phone to my father. Upon hearing it, he became incredibly alarmed and urgently advised me to delete the recording immediately. I complied with his advice and deleted the recording. However, upon restoring and listening to the recording again later, I didn't sense any malice or danger. Rather, I sensed that there was an attempt to make contact with me. At first, I thought extraterrestrials had taken over my session.

The mystery lingered until I underwent a regression hypnosis session with Jeff at a later date. Every single one of my questions was addressed, and my concerns were indeed validated during this session.

14

Past Life as a Squirrel in Norway

As a hypnotherapist and past life regression specialist, I am a passionate seeker of knowledge and thrilling experiences. I love to explore uncharted territories, experiment with different techniques, and uncover hidden truths in my practice. Every session felt like a whimsical journey of discovery, where I was constantly surprised and allowed to unlock the mysteries of the mind.

As I was completing the Quantum Healing Hypnosis program and preparing to start practicing with clients, a friend of mine asked me if I had ever experienced it myself. While I had conducted numerous hypnotherapy sessions and past life regressions, I had yet to undergo quantum healing hypnosis.

As fate would have it, that very night, I discovered a practitioner nearby. Without hesitation, I reached out to him, and to my surprise, someone had just canceled their appointment, making room for me the following day. It felt as if everything was falling into place as if it were meant to be. I must admit I felt a mix of nervousness and excitement. I knew this experience would be mind-blowing. Before embarking on sessions with my clients, I wanted to go through the process myself. I also had several questions about my well-being and personal life that I wanted to explore with the subconscious.

Jeff, the practitioner, and I had a small chat about my life. He asked me what I wanted to achieve and what my intentions were for the session. I also gave him a list of questions I wanted answers to.

Without difficulty, I entered a trance. I found myself in a state of comfort and tranquility, floating on a cloud toward a significant past life. As I descended, I was greeted with a breathtaking scene of lush green fields, majestic trees, and a charming village nestled at the foot of a hill. It was a small village in Norway, and the beauty of the landscape was awe-inspiring. It was a peaceful summer day, and the air was filled with serenity.

I had to ground myself and describe what I saw. To my surprise, I witnessed a transformation from an animal's nails to a baby's feet and back again. I struggled to identify who I was. However, a clear image emerged of me stretching my golden, furry body on a tree.

Initially, I felt disappointed, thinking, "Surely, I have experienced more significant past lives than that of a squirrel in Norway." I was confused. I had seen myself as a more prominent figure in history before. However, I remembered that even the most ordinary and uneventful life can still carry a profound message from the depths of my subconscious. This message may offer valuable insights into my current circumstances.

It did not take long for me to realize that I was living in a hole in the tree next to a small, old house that belonged to an old woman, and she lovingly fed and nurtured me with her own hands. She confided in me, knowing that I would understand. She was an incredibly wise woman, radiating positive energy. Every word she spoke offered guidance and insight that transcended time and space. Her wisdom extended beyond personal matters; she possessed a profound understanding of the world and effortlessly navigated through life.

Next, Jeff instructed me to leave that scene and fast-forward to a significant day, a day that held importance or had something significant happening. I was suddenly back in my house, all by myself, in the dark, and filled with a deep sense of abandonment. It was the day the elderly woman passed away. Her energy was gone, leaving behind an empty house devoid of life and spirit. I felt utterly alone.

As I witnessed this scene, tears welled up in my eyes. The profound sadness and loneliness that permeated the air enveloped me, leaving me overwhelmed with emotion.

In a moment of profound thought, Jeff asked a question that prompted me to stop and contemplate. "Every life carries a lesson and a purpose. What knowledge have you gathered from this experience?" His inquiry sparked a flurry of revelations, astounding me with their depth and significance.

The lessons I learned during my time as a squirrel resonated deeply within me:

- Embrace the freedom that life offers, and don't succumb to the pressures of conformity.
- Take control of your destiny and be the architect of your happiness.
- Let no one dim your inner light, and never forget the power you hold within.
- Write your own story and leave a mark on the world.
- Always remember who you are and what you're capable of.
- Rise above adversity and believe in your limitless potential.

These lessons, born from my unique perspective as a squirrel, hold immense value and can guide me toward a more fulfilling and meaningful existence.

Leaving my previous existence in the rearview, I found myself drawn towards a brilliant white light. I kept going up, higher and higher, until its bright brilliance completely engulfed me. The energy was unique, tranquil, and imbued with a sense of unadulterated love.

I was the one doing it. I had done it before.

My eyes were transfixed on the vast luminosity that lay in front of me. Light beings, resembling small orbs, floated around me. Pure white in color; they weren't exactly orbs but instead concentrated forms of light. They stood out against the light that surrounded me. They simply drifted past me on their serene journey.

J: How vast does this white light reach?

V: It's limitless; there's no end.

J: Do you sense yourself as part of the white light?

V: Yes. It's an amazing feeling of oneness.

J: What do you know about this location?

V: It's a waiting area.

J: What are you waiting for?

V: I'm waiting for the next step.

J: Do you know what the next step is?

V: Yes. We'll likely review my past life.

J: Who will join you in reviewing it?

V: My teachers. I'll meet them soon.

J: Do you have any spirit guides around you?

V: It feels like someone escorted me here but then stepped aside.

J: You mentioned you're going to review your life. Let's advance to the point where you   review your life. You are there now. What do you see?

V: I see a few teachers before me.

J: How many?

V: Three to five.

J: What are they communicating?

V: They are saying it was a short life. I needed it for my next life.

J: What else are they saying?

V: Don't stray from this path. There will be numerous distractions. See the path; follow the path. There will be individuals attempting to take away my motivation and distract me from my life's purpose. In the future, life will be more challenging. More trials, more distractions, and I need to recall the wisdom from the past to identify distractions and overcome hurdles.

J: It seems like a nice review.

V: They're chuckling because they're thrilled about my next life. That was just a warm-up. The real challenges are approaching now, and the true journey is beginning now.

J: Is there any one of those entities that you feel is superior, or do they all feel equal?

V: Archangel Michael is here. He has been supporting me constantly. He believes that I'm ready.

J: Is there anything else they wish to convey before you part with them?

V: Yes. Buckle up! Get ready! It's about to get exciting. Don't fall into despair because nothing seems to be happening at that moment. Gather the energy for the next step, learn to relax, and take breaks because it's merely recharging before the big step. They said I shouldn't get despondent when nothing seems to be progressing in my life, and when I feel stagnant, it's just a preparatory step.

J: Anything else?

V: They're proud of me. I've lived a good life... But they're laughing about what's going to happen to me next. They said that I had no idea what I had signed up for. They're saying they might grab some popcorn because it's going to get interesting. They're teasing me.

J: They do have a sense of humor. Don't they? They're very loving.

V: They also said, "You are never alone on this journey. We will be with you every step of the way, guiding you and nudging you in the right direction. Trust in yourself and the wisdom you have gained."

Meeting My Soul Group

With those words, a sense of calm washed over me. I knew that even though the challenges might be daunting, I had the inner strength to overcome them. The love and support that surrounded me in this realm reassured me that I was never alone.

After my encounter with my guides, I proceeded to meet my soul group. These were beings with whom I shared a deep spiritual connection, a collective consciousness. Being in their presence was like reuniting with a long-lost family; a profound sense of love and familiarity enveloped me.

J: Can you provide a more detailed description of them?

V: It appears they're engrossed in social interaction and are enjoying themselves.

J: Are any of them identifiable to you?

V: None specifically, but I do have a sense of familiarity with them.

J: Select one that stands out and describe it to me.

V: A charming young man approaches; he recognizes me and invites me to join them.

J: Can you tell me more about him? Do you remember him from this life?

V: I'm uncertain, but I believe he might be my soulmate, whom I've yet to encounter. But I'm unsure. He's a good person, indeed.

J: Who else is present?

V: My grandmother is somewhere here. She's part of my group.

J: Do you know the number of individuals in your group, your soul family?

V: Including this man, there are seven or eight of us.

J: And you've all been together for quite a while?

V: Yes, but we don't always reincarnate together in each lifetime. Sometimes, someone will choose not to return, so we take breaks from Earth. At times, they accompany me, and we discover each other in our respective lives if we reincarnate in the same lifetime.

J: Are you all following the same path, or are your paths different?

V: It varies. Not always. Some of us have our own lessons to learn in different lives, independent of me.

J: But generally, you all belong to one soul group, right?

V: Yes, that's correct.

J: What is your main area of study?

V: Our goal is to go to Earth, remember who we are, and teach others. Then we regroup and reflect on our lessons, trying to better ourselves and avoid repeating mistakes. We discuss the distractions on Earth that might prevent us from awakening. We also discuss those who fail to awaken and why that happens. Everything is a test. We come to Earth to pass a test. When we reunite, we analyze and discuss what led to failure and how we can prevent that from happening again. Then, we guide others on what to avoid and how to improve so they can awaken.

J: Do you impart these teachings while you're on Earth or back home?

V: My mission is primarily focused on Earth. We simply share our knowledge when we are back there. We all have a metaphorical 'backpack' filled with tools. When you come to Earth, you're given this 'backpack' to maintain your connection with the spirit world. If you feel disconnected, you can use these tools to reconnect and remember your true self. However, some souls fail to use it, leading to their inability to awaken. But that, too, is a lesson for them.

J: How can they access their 'backpacks'?

V: They need to quiet their minds. They need to disconnect from distractions and noises, spend more time in nature, meditate, do breathwork, be around waterfalls, visit the ocean and mountains, and listen to high-frequency music. All these activities help soothe their minds. When they connect to themselves, they reestablish this connection. This makes it easier to recall why they came here. It's similar to a newborn kitten, who is initially blind but gradually gains sight. Some people die blind, never gaining sight.

J: Yes, it's important. What is the most important thing they explain to you?

V: Always remember where you came from.

That's how you know your way; you exit through the same path you came in. Knowledge on Earth is very important for the next stage. It's essential to evolve and experience the Earth's existence because it's not only a form of entertainment but also a school and lesson for our soul's evolution. There are so many distractions—darkness, violence, anger, and fear—on Earth, and it's very easy to get swept off your feet and to flow into darkness. But those who stand their ground, discover the truth, and see through the illusions are the ones who are going to teach others.

J: Do you know how many lives you've lived on Earth?

V: I am not sure if it was every century, but I'm sure I've been here from the very beginning of everything. I have seen every step of evolution on Earth.

J: Have you ever lived somewhere other than Earth?

V: Yes, other planets.

J: Please tell me about those.

V: It's different from Earth. I don't know what kind of planet it is, but it looks darker than I see in space.

J: So how is it different?

V: There is less life, less wildlife, and fewer beings. It's hard to survive there; it's not like on Earth. I don't think there are any animals.

J: Would you prefer to incarnate there or on Earth?

V: No, there's nothing to do there. The souls go there to learn lessons, but as soon as they learn them, they leave because there's nothing to do and no fun. It's just like a stepping stone for the soul's evolution—a quick test.

The final phase of the session was dedicated to establishing a connection with SC, or the subconscious, for answers to my queries and overall health improvement. While some refer to it as the subconscious, others have known it as the source, universal energy, divine energy, the energy of the creator, oneness, or the higher soul. Regardless, it doesn't have a definitive term, as it signifies collective energy.

J: Could you please scan her body? Is there anything that requires our focus?

SC: There is an energy block in her chest.

J: Is there anything we can do to alleviate this immediately?

SC: Yes. (I was breathing heavily for a bit.)

J: It's disappeared; what's next?

SC: There's a concern in her lower abdomen.

J: Is it something you can handle?

SC: Yes.

J: Can you provide healing for her reproductive area? What did you discover there?

SC: More energy blocks, but they're not severe; they can be easily cleared.

J: So you're able to clear them out?

SC: Yes.

J: I'm really curious about how it works. Can you explain it to me?

SC: I'm sending energy to her stomach. She's doing Reiki herself, and she is doing great. But she doesn't do it every night, but she should.

J: Can you explain how she can do it?

SC: She knows she should do it, but she doesn't do it enough. She only does it sometimes, but she needs to do it every night.

J: It's like a form of meditation or something she does with her energy. How does it work?

SC: All she needs to do is listen to high-vibration music. It will vibrate and help her heal naturally. It will also help her feel better and be in her element. It will also help her stay balanced. Then she will know what to do next. She knows how to do it.

J: Thank you, thank you so much for your assistance. One of the topics she raised concerned the information she has been uncovering about her past lives. She contemplates whether to share this knowledge through a book or articles or keep it to herself. What course of action should she take?

SC: She has already taken the first steps by writing articles, and we couldn't be prouder of her. She can continue to write piece by piece, knowing that eventually, they will find their way into the world. Some may be published, while others may not, but through this process, she can introduce people to the incredible world of hypnosis and past life regression and share her personal experiences.

Many individuals are drawn to learn and practice quantum healing hypnosis, and by sharing articles and personal stories, she can spread this message to the masses and prepare them for the next stage of our collective evolution. This is the same mission that you and other practitioners are undertaking. She is making remarkable progress and has discovered a hidden talent for writing that she never knew she possessed.

J: It's truly remarkable. I've noticed that a significant number of us in this generation are being called to engage in this type of work. Even I have felt the pull towards this path, as have many of my peers. Could there be a larger shift happening that is inspiring this desire within us?

SC: The universe has called upon you, and you have answered that call. That's what it is. You have awakened to your purpose, just like others who are experiencing their awakening. They feel the calling and are instinctively drawn to practitioners like you and me, seeking to awaken their latent abilities and fulfill their life's purpose. We all agreed to undertake this journey. It's not a new concept to us; it's more like a familiar blanket. You were living your human life, and then the calling resonated within you. Suddenly, everything fell into place, and you became aware of your life's purpose: to help others awaken, heal, and believe. In due time, you will also write a book to further inspire and guide others on their transformative journeys.

I was given excellent ideas for enhancing my daily life and a detailed plan for my hypnotherapy practice. The subconscious also taught me that there is a reason why we are here. I would be able to hear my inner guidance if I tried to quiet my mind, meditate, go to the beach, spend time in nature, and practice breathwork. I was reminded to stay on course and not get sidetracked by nearby sounds. My inner self held all the answers to my inquiries.

However, the most significant question was also resolved: Was my session taken over by extraterrestrials? The response and its validation were astonishing.

J: There were just a few more questions she had. During a hypnosis session, she started hearing this weird noise in her headphones. She actually played it to me today before our session. Can you tell her what it was?

SC: It is coding.

J: What?

SC: It's coding. A coded message from another universe, another planet, to remind her where she's coming from. Now, she's living an earthly experience, and they wanted her to keep this connection to another planet. That other planet has a missing puzzle piece in her game in this life. There's nothing that she can understand with her conscious mind. Nobody can explain, neither you, nor the teacher, nor her father. Her father got scared, but she had subconsciously the knowledge that she needed to keep this message. It's also ingrained in her DNA that when she's going to need something, it's going to come automatically. It's the knowledge you cannot get from your experience, nor is it the knowledge that we can provide. It's the knowledge you can only get from this planet, and this is an amazing puzzle in her game here in life. She is going to use it when it's needed, so there's nothing you can describe with words or symbols. There is no description of it. It's nothing bad; it's a good thing. Yes, the session got hijacked; this is true, but it was the only way for that planet to communicate with her because otherwise, she could mess it up a little bit without that missing knowledge.

J: Okay...thank you. Does she have anyone in her life now or in the future who will be there to support her and help her through the tough times?

SC: She has strong support from us. She can easily reach out to us whenever she needs to because we are constantly communicating with her. Whether she's meditating or just staying quiet, she can hear and understand our messages clearly. And if she ever needs assistance or wants to do some research, all she has to do is ask us.

J: That's truly amazing. Being able to hear you directly is a special gift. In her sleep, she feels that someone is working on her body.

SC: That's us.

J: What are you working on?

SC: What she destroyed during the day, we need to restore during the night.

J: She sees you scaring away.

SC: Yes.

J: I thought it was rather amusing.

And she said she saw something above her dresser at night. Could you tell her what it was?

SC: We were teaching her to work with energy. That's what she saw above her desk. We showed her how to manipulate the energy with her hands, and that's when she saw the light ball between somebody's hands. We were just teaching her. She's going to know what to do. Subconsciously, it is all recorded. She is going to use it when it's needed, and it's going to come naturally. It's in her DNA.

J: Yeah, she was telling me about it. It is so fascinating. Is there anything specific you would like to ask on her behalf or provide an answer for?

SC: She has an additional inquiry from her list, which revolves around her family in Europe. She willingly chose this family, having signed up for it. However, they are not her soul tribe; they merely serve as a surrogate family. When she decided to leave not just her family but also her home country, she followed her instincts. They, too, are evolving and learning their lessons through her personal growth.

J: Thank you for your insight. Before concluding this session, do you have any final thoughts or messages you would like to convey to her?

SC: She is destined for greatness—on a grand scale. We are here to support her wholeheartedly; she possesses vast knowledge and resources. What she needs is to believe in herself and release any self-destructive thoughts that occasionally plague her mind, leading her to doubt the authenticity of her experiences. Everything she encounters is real; she possesses a deep understanding of her purpose. Our connection with her is strong, and she must strive to maintain a high vibrational state. She learned a valuable lesson the hard way, as we demonstrated that she could have it all, only to take it away abruptly, leaving her feeling helpless. However, this was a necessary lesson to reinforce the importance of maintaining a high vibrational state. Spending more time in nature and visiting the ocean will greatly benefit her. She will find her love soon. She's also skeptical about this. And the person she is thinking of is the one she's going to meet soon.

J: Excellent. Thank you for all the information you have given us today. Thank you.

As I slowly emerged from the deep state of hypnosis, I felt a profound sense of gratitude for the experience I had just undergone. It was like peering into the depths of my soul and receiving guidance from the wisest parts of myself. I knew that this session had unlocked a hidden treasure within me, revealing profound lessons and insights that would shape my present and future.

In the days that followed, I reflected on the messages and lessons I had received. The simplicity and yet profound wisdom of my past life as a squirrel in Norway resonated deeply with me. It reminded me to embrace my uniqueness, to trust my instincts, and to create my path in life, regardless of what others may think or expect. The passing of the elderly woman in that past life taught me the importance of cherishing the connections we have with others and the impact we can have on their lives. It reminded me to appreciate the wisdom and guidance of those who come into our lives, even if they may seem insignificant or unconventional.

As I connected with my guides in the realm of pure love and light, I felt a renewed sense of purpose and determination. I knew that the challenges that lay ahead would test me, but I also knew that I had the strength and support to overcome them. I also realized that crossing that fine line toward positive life changes requires a willingness to explore new paths, embrace uncertainty, and trust in the process.

We must venture outside of our comfort zones for it and be open to the lessons and messages that come our way, even if they seem insignificant or nonsensical at first. I believe that by embracing change, trusting in ourselves, and staying open to new possibilities, we can all cross that fine line toward a better version of ourselves and create the lives we truly desire.

15

A Spontaneous Trip to Mount Shasta

Mount Shasta is a majestic and mystical mountain located in northern California, known for its spiritual significance and magical energies. It is one of the most powerful energy vortexes on the planet, attracting seekers, healers, and spiritual pilgrims from around the world. Due to the minimal barrier between the physical and spiritual dimensions, connecting with higher realms becomes more straightforward.

Mount Shasta is home to a hidden city of light, Telos. It is described as a thriving underground city inhabited by an ancient race of beings known as the Lemurians, who are considered to be the descendants of the lost continent of Lemuria.

Legend has it that Telos is a place of advanced technology, spiritual enlightenment, and harmonious living. The

Lemurians live in perfect harmony with nature and each other, embodying principles of love, peace, and unity. Telos is believed to serve as a spiritual haven and healing center for those seeking wisdom, guidance, and transformation.

The myth of Telos continues to fascinate and inspire those who are drawn to the mysteries of Mount Shasta and the ancient wisdom of the Lemurian civilization.

As I prepared for my upcoming journey, the sky gifted me with a rainbow each day, a symbol of beauty and hope. The colorful arcs appeared to carry whispers of the exciting adventures that lay ahead, foreshadowing the extraordinary story that was about to unravel. It served as a reassuring reminder that even during darkness, there was always a glimmer of light and optimism waiting to break through.

Even if just one cloud lingered on the horizon, a rainbow would emerge like a sign from my guides. I could feel their unwavering support in those colorful arcs stretching across the sky. It was as if they reminded me that no matter what challenges I faced, they were always there to guide and protect me. The rainbow was a beautiful reminder that I was never alone and that my guides would always be there to light my path through the storm.

While walking with my dog one day, I looked up to see the rainbow again. I was filled with a deep sense of love and encouragement in that instant. The divine sign inspired me to act, and I hurried home to book my trip to Mt. Shasta for the next day. It felt as if everything was falling into place with lightning speed.

Setting off bright and early the following morning, I began my adventure with my faithful companion Kiki by my side. This beloved dog had been my constant companion on countless journeys, accompanying me as we explored the length and breadth of the country, creating treasured memories with each passing mile.

The drive from Los Angeles up to the Sacramento area proved to be quite challenging for me. The stagnant energy weighed heavily on my spirit, leaving me feeling drowsy and fatigued. I couldn't help but blame myself for embarking on such a lengthy trip. However, as I passed Sacramento, the scenery transformed, and a renewed sense of vitality washed over me. I began to enjoy the ride when I saw wisps of clouds accompanied by the golden tones of autumn trees reflected in serene lakes. It felt almost mesmerizing as if I had stepped into a fairytale realm inhabited by elves and fairies. As the road wound closer to Mt. Shasta, ascending the hills, the breathtaking views from above stole my breath away.

I arrived at Mount Shasta just before sunset. The energy enveloped me, reminding me of the familiar embrace I had felt in Sedona. It felt like coming home. Exhausted yet serene, I settled into the peacefulness of the surroundings.

The following day, I took my dog for a walk and grabbed a strong cup of coffee from a local shop next door. A profound sense of wholeness washed over me as if I had found my rightful place in the world. The first item on my agenda was a visit to Lake Siskiyou, a reservoir located in Siskiyou County, California. The lake is surrounded by beautiful forest scenery, making it a picturesque destination for outdoor enthusiasts.

I got there early and was at peace by myself. A sense of unity and togetherness filled the air. I basked in the serenity, watching the clouds dance upon the mountain, their reflection shimmering in the crystal-clear water. It was a picture-perfect scene that captivated my senses. At that moment, I couldn't help but express gratitude to the creator for the beauty that enveloped us and for this magnificent masterpiece we call Earth. Numerous undiscovered treasures are just waiting to be found, and so many awe-inspiring places remain unknown to us.

The majority of our lives are confined inside our comfort zones. We create these boxes for ourselves to live and work in, which leaves little opportunity to fully appreciate the wonders of life beyond. However, the real magic happens when we step outside the box and discover the extraordinary.

I was spoiled by the harmony and beauty of nature while I was growing up in a small Eastern European country. It served as a continual reminder of my carefree youth when I would go for walks in the forest with friends and enjoy the clean air. I cannot help but get jealous sometimes of our ease and independence during those days spent in the woods. I am incredibly appreciative of the chance to take in the wild beauty of village life, complete with fields, forests, wild animals, and birds. Looking back now, it feels like a luxurious escape from the chaotic pace of city life.

But as the years went by, I decided to leave my homeland behind. I found myself drawn to the allure of big cities like Hamburg in Germany, Los Angeles, Houston, and Miami. Each city had its own unique charm, captivating me in different ways. However, none of them could compare to the magical scenery of solitude—just me and a serene lake in a forest accompanied by my dog. This newfound luxury became my sanctuary, a place to escape the hustle and bustle of the city and the heavy traffic.

The morning was chilly, and Kiki wasn't too thrilled about the weather. So, I left her at the hotel and ventured off to the mountain alone. The day was really cold but sunny, just before the arrival of the first snowstorm. The road leading up to the mountain was awe-inspiring, and I couldn't help but enjoy the ride. I sang along to the music in my car, taking in the beauty that surrounded me. Unfortunately, the icy conditions prevented me from reaching the mountain's summit, and I parked my car and observed the activities of other visitors. Some people were meditating, others were hiking, and a few were busy capturing pictures. As I observed these diverse activities, I felt reassured that I was exactly where I needed to be at that moment.

Despite a nagging toothache, I refused to let it dampen my spirits. I must admit, I felt a bit lost, unsure of what to do during my time on the mountain. I found a cold stone to sit on, attempting to meditate. However, the stone's freezing temperature forced me to keep moving. I chose a direction and started walking, hoping to find some clarity.

Venturing deeper into the forest, a profound sense of solitude surrounded me as no other presence interrupted my journey. Suddenly, my eyes were drawn to a mesmerizing sight: two trees intertwined at their roots, growing as a unified entity. I was deeply moved by the scene and felt compelled to record the occasion with photos and videos. It was as they were saying: "We are you. You are us. We are one." Overwhelmed with emotion, I found myself hugging each tree, feeling the masculine and feminine energies they exuded. It was a powerful union, nestled in the heart of nowhere or perhaps the very center of everything.

Lost in this moment of connection, a woman with a British accent approached me, witnessing my interaction with nature. Despite a fleeting sense of embarrassment, I greeted her warmly and shared my observation about the trees resembling twin flames. She agreed, mentioning her prior visits to this spot and exuding a sense of familiarity with the surroundings. As she continued her solitary hike, I admired her fearless spirit, realizing that I, too, possessed the courage to explore these enchanting paths alone.

As I continued my journey through the forest, my mood lifted. The snow beneath my feet felt a little icy. I found solace in capturing the beauty of the surroundings through my camera lens. Like a carefree child, I reveled in the untamed wilderness that surrounded me, experiencing a newfound sense of freedom and happiness. The energy of the natural realm was nothing short of magnificent, and the snow-covered peak of the mountain held a captivating allure. I spent hours exploring the landscape, capturing the play of light and shadow and the majestic wildlife that roamed free. As I hiked higher, I felt a rush of adrenaline and excitement. The crisp air filled my lungs, and the view took my breath away.

Yearning to connect with the spiritual realms of St. Germain and Adama, I encountered a barrier that prevented me from fully communicating with them.

Entering a trance-like state usually came naturally to me, allowing me to let go and connect. However, this time, I struggled to reach that state, leaving me slightly frustrated. The persistent toothache added to my discomfort. Determined to find solace, I continued walking, channeling Reiki energy into my being. Normally, this practice would quickly transport me to a state of tranquility. Step by step, I moved forward, pausing intermittently to close my eyes and take a few more steps. Then, a voice echoed in my mind, instructing me to turn back once I finished with Reiki.

Upon reviewing the pictures I had taken, a revelation struck me. Almost every snapshot captured the subtle radiance of a violet sphere with a blue mark at the edge, shining close to my cheek in perfect alignment with the prior location of my ache. It was a tiny yet irrefutable entity, casting a soft glow of blue-violet luminance on my cheek. Astonishingly, the pain had vanished, slipping from my memory until I returned to my hotel room.

In my perception, the shade of violet mirrored the transformational might of Saint Germain's Violet Flame, while the touch of blue mirrored Adama's, the Blue Ray, essential nature. Both are spiritual entities that have left significant imprints on humanity's guidance and protection throughout history.

Adama is a revered spiritual figure, believed to be the High Priest of the ancient civilization of Lemuria. Following the demise of Lemuria, Adama and his followers retreated to an ethereal city beneath Mount Shasta, known as Telos, the City of Light.

Conversely, Saint Germain is a mythical character who has lived through numerous lifetimes and attained enlightenment. He is frequently linked with alchemy, spiritual metamorphosis, and the Violet Flame, believed to convert negative energy into positive. Saint Germain is also thought to be a master among the ascended masters, a collection of highly advanced spiritual entities that shepherd humanity toward elevated consciousness levels.

The realization dawned on me that I had indeed had a profound encounter with both entities. Deep within, I knew the truth.

16

Connection to Lemuria and Mount Shasta

On the way back to Los Angeles a profound sense of anticipation washed over me. It was as if the universe whispered that my return to Mt. Shasta would not be far off and that this next visit would unveil hidden mysteries previously concealed from my understanding. The time was ripe for discovery, and I eagerly embraced the path that lay ahead.

In LA I participated in a group meditation aimed at exploring the Akashic records even more. I had two specific questions that I wanted to have answered. The first question concerned my recurrent dreams, which I firmly feel have something to do with the collapse of the lost continent of Lemuria. In these dreams, I always see a huge wave heading toward the land, and then I see it all from above as the water swallows everything up and nothing is to save. It was all gone. I yearned to understand the significance and meaning behind these dreams, as well as their connection to Lemuria's demise.

The second question stemmed from a curious encounter where someone mentioned that if I feel a strong pull towards Mount Shasta, as I undeniably do, it might indicate the presence of someone awaiting me there. Intrigued by this possibility, I aimed to uncover any information regarding my past experiences during the time of Lemuria and identify the individual who might be patiently waiting for me on Mount Shasta.

So with a set intention, I started my journey, I found myself in a magnificent large library. As I took in the surroundings, a young girl of around ten, but with wisdom beyond her years, approached me and warmly greeted me. She softly grasped my hand and urged me to follow her. Together, we passed through a doorway of shimmering golden light. The little child changed dramatically as soon as we stepped inside the door. She now appeared to be a little girl of five to six years old, radiating an aura of wisdom and familiarity.

Momentarily taken aback, I paused to gather my thoughts. Sensing my hesitation, she looked at me with a cute smile and affectionately called me "mom," inviting me to join her. As the little girl continued to play, I felt a surge of curiosity and asked her about the person waiting for me on Mt. Shasta, in Telos. To my surprise, she responded with a confident "yes" and referred to him as her daddy. I was curious, so I followed up to find out what had happened to me. With a serene expression, she explained that during the fall of Lemuria, both she and I lost our lives and went underwater. However, her daddy had moved to Telos and had been patiently waiting for us to realign ever since.

For the reunion to take place, she said that I needed to raise my vibration. She mentioned that she was currently in an Angel Realm, while I was still experiencing life in 3-D. To reunite with her daddy, I needed to elevate my vibration and transcend the limitations of the physical plane.

I asked her about her father's name. But suddenly, my critical mind began to interject, bombarding me with various names and causing confusion. Sensing my internal struggle, the little girl paused. At that very moment, I sensed a comforting and familiar energy standing behind me. The powerful presence almost swallowed me with its intensity. A feeling of love surrounded me, along with a soothing voice that affectionately called me "darling." It seemed as though this presence had been silently by my side, offering unwavering support and helping to lift my spirits.

The voice assured me that indeed, he has been helping me every step of the way, guiding me towards higher consciousness and aligning our vibrations for our eventual reunion. He emphasized that he had been helping me choose the path of greater knowledge and love by giving me little prods, synchronicities, and inspirational moments.

Tears welled up in my eyes as I realized the magnitude of this support. It was a profound realization that I was not alone on this journey and that there was a divine force looking out for me and guiding me toward a reunion with my counterpart from the past. It was clear that the process of raising my vibration was not just for my benefit but for the greater purpose of reuniting with my family and soul companions and experiencing the love and support that had been missing in this lifetime.

I understood that the journey toward higher consciousness was not just about personal growth but also about reconnecting with the deep bonds that transcend time and space. It was a reminder that we are never truly alone and that there are forces at play, both seen and unseen, guiding us towards love, compassion, and unity.

As I reflected on the profound experiences and revelations of the meditation, I acknowledged that there was still much work to be done on myself. The journey toward higher consciousness and reunion with my counterpart was not a destination but an ongoing process of self-discovery and growth. I understood that to fully align with my true self and raise my vibration, I needed to delve deeper into my inner workings. This meant exploring my fears, limiting beliefs, and patterns that no longer served me. It meant embracing vulnerability and facing the shadows within me with compassion and understanding.

I also recognized the importance of self-care and self-love in this transformative journey. Taking the time to nurture my physical, mental, and emotional well-being was essential for my growth and the elevation of my energy. This meant establishing healthy boundaries, practicing mindfulness, and participating in things that made me happy and fulfilled. This process was not just about achieving perfec-

tion or reaching a final destination but rather about embracing the continuous evolution of my being.

17

Mount Shasta is Calling

Interestingly, during my journey back to LA, I had a lingering feeling that I would return to Mt. Shasta for an extended period. Though I initially dismissed the thought, over time, I found myself drawn to information about Adama and Telos, receiving his telepathic messages. He began preparing me to spend time on Mt. Shasta to write not only one but two books. Initially, I doubted my ability to accomplish this assignment, given that English isn't my native language and my writing experience is limited. I thought, "You, guys, have a great sense of humor".

But despite my doubts, I had already envisioned the titles and covers for my two books, and they resonated deeply with me. This recollection brought me back to a regression hypnosis session with Jeff the previous summer, where the subconscious encouraged me to write. Both my father and sister are writers, and even my mother has authored a few articles. I was the only one hesitating, questioning my capabilities.

After contemplating for a few days, I decided, "Why not?" It felt like the universe had presented me with an opportunity, and it sounded like an adventurous project. With my lease ending in the summer and a sense of freedom, I embraced the challenge and chose to embark on this writing journey.

After I made up my mind to go to Mt. Shasta, I started to receive more information on how to prepare for it. I began attracting people with valuable tips and information, and I also came across Paul of Venus. I will write about my experience with him in my next book. I also started getting more insides from Adama, and he wanted me to gather all available information on how to write a book quickly. He suggested bringing a recorder to record messages and finding an app that could transcribe the recordings into text. This approach seemed promising, and with support, I realized it was possible.

As I started making a solid to-do list, my doubts began to fade away. I researched the area for short-term rentals and tours. I was advised that for the first three days, I needed to clear the old energy from LA by relaxing, walking, and meditating. On the third day, I was supposed to do a four-hour tour with Paul of Venus and visit the Telos Portal. The writing process would commence on the fourth day with new energy and readiness. I was instructed to get water from a natural spring and avoid sugar and meat, among other requirements. Each day, I was to visit different places to get in a receptive state and receive messages from Adama, who had valuable information to share, and I was chosen to do it.

As I delved deeper into the topic, I began mentally packing my belongings and planning the big move. I discovered other books written in Mt. Shasta by authors who felt a similar calling. Some had relocated permanently, while others stayed for a month or a few months to finish writing. However, we all shared the common experience of being called and accepting that call.

The excitement was growing bigger with each passing day. Everything was unfolding fast. I knew the preparation was going on at full speed. They (my spirit guides) were not kidding, so neither was I. It felt like the right thing to do for me. I felt like I was coming closer to discovering who I am and my history.

But as I settled in to begin writing the chapter, a wave of doubt crept in, causing me to question my capabilities for the task ahead. Thoughts of whether I was truly prepared or if there might be a better candidate for the job started swirling in my mind. Just then, a telepathic message from Adama pierced through my doubts, sensing my uncertainty and offering a reassuring presence:

"My darling, you are doing the right thing. You were chosen because we know that you are the right person for it. Don't worry; you have our support and protection. You are divinely guided. Together, we have a huge project ahead of us. You have been prepared for it for years. You are ready. And you will be fine. Adama."

My cheeks flushed with embarrassment as he discovered me lost in my negative thoughts, tears welling in my eyes. However, his message radiated love, care, and support, reassuring me that I had a strong pillar of support to lean on as I tackled this daunting project.

I find great comfort in the way my spirit guides call me "darling." It fills me with a sense of security and protection, making me feel never alone. This endearing term first started being used around the time I was planning my trip to Mount Shasta last year. It's a small gesture that brings me immense warmth and reassurance, especially in times of uncertainty. I am grateful to have spirit guides who show such love and care towards me, always ensuring that I am safe and supported. Each time I hear them say "darling," it reminds me of the unique connection we have and the unwavering love they have for me. I feel truly fortunate to have such a nurturing and loving presence in my life.

18

Past Life as Madame de Pompadour

It had been some time since my introductory regression session with Jeff. I had new queries and life challenges that I sought insight on. This led me to cross paths with Charbel, another amazing and gifted practitioner.

The following day, I reached out to Charbel and asked if he was open to doing a session. To my delight, he agreed, and we booked an appointment for the following weekend. The anticipation was overwhelming as I counted down the days until my session. I was excited but also somewhat nervous. My first quantum healing hypnosis with Jeff had been a profound experience, and I wasn't sure what to expect this time.

On the morning of the session, I began envisioning the kind of past life I desired to witness. I wished to see how Elizabeth secretly gave birth to her son. But quickly I realized I was attempting to control the session and needed to let go. I understand that we must trust our subconscious to choose our past lives, and we need to trust that it knows what we need to see and why. This is the advice I share with my clients: not to try to dictate the session but to trust the process and let it unfold. I caught myself controlling the session in my mind. It was unusual for me. I decided to follow my own advice and let go of all the preconceived notions.

Upon my arrival at the destination, the atmosphere instantly evoked a sense of home. The surroundings were warm and inviting, aesthetically arranged to suit the upcoming regression session. To help me unwind and soothe my senses, I was presented with a cup of calming herbal tea. In anticipation of the unfamiliarity of the new place, I had packed my cherished pair of warm socks to foster a sense of comfort.

In our dialogue, we delved into the complexities and queries concerning my present life. Strangely, though, I overlooked discussing my past life as Madame de Pompadour, and no questions were raised about it either. The truth was, I didn't seek any validation concerning that life, as its clarity was already engraved in my mind. My curiosity and questions were solely directed towards Elizabeth I. My fascination with her life, her power, and the challenges she faced was something I needed to understand, and I knew this session would provide the answers I sought.

The room was dimly lit and quiet. I closed my eyes, took a deep breath, and tried to clear my mind. I started to relax. I could feel my heartbeat slowing down, and I felt a sense of calm wash over me. I knew I needed to trust my subconscious and let it lead me through this journey. As his voice started to guide me toward profound tranquility, I could sense my awareness fading, transcending the boundaries of time and space. Concurrently, Dolores Cannon's voice seamlessly entered the session, echoing the same words as Charbel. Initially, I was uncertain about who to pay attention to, but then I realized it didn't matter.

With each passing moment, I could feel the connection with my current life fading away, replaced by images and sensations from a completely different era. I felt as though I was speeding through the air, similar to an airplane coming in for a landing. Everything below me blurred into a single streak due to my speed. But as my pace started to reduce, I could make out the green fields and the road below.

Another Meeting With Madame

C: What do you see down there below?

V: Greenfield... summertime...a lot of green grass and the road. I just saw the carriage pass by, I think with four horses and with bells. I don't see it anymore.

C: Is there anyone driving this carriage?

V: Yes. I think there was a lady...in a carriage. The type of carriage that can be unfolded for the summer.

C: Are you already in a physical body?

V: I am kind of standing by the side and absorbing this carriage.

C: Do you have a body?

V: I want to slip into that lady's body. I don't know why.

C: So you are absorbing the scene?

V: Yes. I am absorbing from above, but I have the feeling it's my body.

C: Can you look down and see if you have feet?

V: Yes, I see pointed shoes with feathers on the side.

C: What are you wearing?

V: Something fluffy, like wide fabric with a lot of volume around the arms and tight around the wrists.

C: Do you feel the body is male or female?

V: Female.

C: Young or old?

V: Young-ish.

C: What are you doing in that field?

V: We are going somewhere...We are driving...we are on the way somewhere.

C: Do you know where you are going?

V: It's a long way; I can't see. We're going to visit someone.

C: Are you still on the way?

V: We are approaching some kind of structure. A big building, like a castle, with a huge stone   wall. What I see is a protective wall, and you need to go through the gate to go inside.

C: Are you married?

V: I don't feel like it. I am feeling a little flirty.

C: What was the color of the dress that you were wearing?

V: The sleeves are white. I see cleavage...nice bust... a tight cream-colored dress.

C: Is it a fitted dress?

V: It is fitted on the top, but from the waist down, it is going fluffier, and with volume, it is a long one. I'm not sure, but I think I see the life of Madame de Pompadour. That Rococo.

At that moment, I felt a little bit confused. Why was I being shown the same past life that I had seen before? I was aware of my past life as Madame de Pompadour, and I didn't need proof of that. However, there must have been a reason why the subconscious was showing me this exact past life but in a different setting.

C: Have you been there before?

V: Yeah, I had a life there that I am aware of. Based on the dress and carriage, it might be it.

C: Let's move backward to before that happened and see what got you into this situation. We are moving backward now, and you can tell me about it. You are there now. What do you see?

V: I'm alone somewhere, walking. Forest or field...forest. I have no idea what I'm doing there by myself.

C: What is there around you?

V: Nothing. Just wildness. I'm singing. It feels like I am flirty...bubbly...bubbly and flirty, that kind of...maybe silly, but smart. I think I have a plan. I don't know why.

C: Do you know what the plan is?

V: No, but I'm feeling very intellectual and wise, and I am using my fluffiness for something. I don't know what yet.

C: You don't know what you're doing there?

V: I have a feeling that I have a plan, but I don't see any-body. In my mind, I have a plan. I am singing and just being happy.

I was instructed to leave that scene and move to another important day.

C: What is happening?

V: I am part of the kin...I am in the castle.

C: Are you already inside of it?

V: Yeah, I am one of them. I live there.

C: What do you do there?

V: I think the plan I was thinking about has worked out perfectly.

C: So, what were you thinking about in terms of how to get inside the castle?

V: I don't know. But it seems the plan has already worked out. What I wanted to do. Now that I am in this palace or castle, I am very important...one of the important people in the castle. She is dressed nicely. Wealthy.

C: Do you know where this castle is located?

V: It comes to mind that it's Versailles, the Palace of Ver-sailles. I see gardens in front of it.

C: Describe the gardens for me.

V: Well-kept, when you see the palace from afar, a well-kept beautiful garden, green beautiful trees, and all together with a garden palace make a beautiful, almost surreal pic-ture.

C: Are you alone? By yourself now?

V: Now, when I'm looking at the palace from the side, I am alone, yes...but it seems like the adrenaline is kicking in because the vibe is different. It's a higher level than I had before. It's almost giving me shivers that my plan worked out. And I got it.

C: So, what was the plan?

V: I think...to get into the royalty life or something.

C: Are you married?

V: No. I have a lover.

C: Does he live in the castle?

V: Yes.

C: What does he do in the castle?

V: He is a king.

C: So, are you a mistress?

V: Yes.

C: Do you have a name?

V: Yes. Madame de Pompadour.

C: How did you get to meet a king?

V: In the forest, in the bush where I was.

C: How did you meet him?

V: Being silly...he paid attention to my silliness. Being fluffy and flirty, just enjoying myself. That's what caught his attention.

C: What's the king's name?

V: Louis.

C: What is the number?

V: XV.

C: Are you happy?

V: Yeah.

C: That's what you wanted?

V: Kind of. I had to sacrifice some things.

C: What did you have to sacrifice?

V: My daughter.

At that moment, tears welled up in my eyes, and feelings of guilt washed over me. I became overwhelmed with emotions, and my voice became shaky.

C: You had a daughter?

V: Yes.

In my mind, I saw a portrait of a little girl with rounded cheeks, and I had the feeling that this was my nephew in my current life, my godson.

C: Was she from a previous marriage?

V: Yes. The king didn't accept her. When I was accepted to be his mistress, I already had a little girl, and I brought her to the palace. He didn't show his disapproval, but he did everything to push the child away and get her out of the way. He was kind of jealous that I spent some time with my daughter.

C: What happened to the father of your daughter?

V: We got divorced, he just stayed out of the scene. He could not do anything against the king. He just accepted it.

C: And what happened to your daughter?

V: She was sent to school, but the main reason was just to get her out of sight.

C: Were you able to see her or check on her?

V: No, I was involved in the court. I had things to do; I had responsibilities. I didn't give much time to my child.

C: How does it make you feel?

V: Horrible.

C: So, you never married the king?

V: No. He was married.

C: So you were only a mistress?

V: Yes. Kind of a favorite mistress.

As the scene shifted to another significant moment in the life we were observing, my attention was immediately drawn to a unique piece of adornment. Instead of the usual jewelry, it was a delicate woven fabric accessory with pearls designed to accentuate the cleavage, adding a touch of elegance and charm to any special occasion. I'm not entirely certain if I can take credit for this masterpiece, as I only truly saw its beauty when I carefully draped it around someone's neck to admire how it looked.

C: Are you still living in the castle?

V: Yeah.

C: How old are you now?

V: 38.

C: How long have you been there for?

V: Not sure, but it feels like home. I have been there for a while, and it feels like I know everything already and how it works.

C: Is there anybody who is causing your problems?

V: Yeah, some people don't like my attitude. I don't pay attention to them. I just do my job because I have the support of the king. So they're just obstacles. Some people don't agree with my vision, and since the king is also observing my vision and projecting it to others, they see me as a bad influence. Not always, but in some parts, yes. The king appreciates my vision, respects it, and listens to it.

C: Do you love the king?

V: We do have a connection, but it's more like a flirtatious one. I do like him, but I don't love him. I like him a lot, and he feels very close to me, but there is another part: I'm doing it for a reason.

C: Are you still in love with the father of your daughter?

V: I feel sorry for him.

C: Have you loved him?

V: It was more like childish love. Not sure.

C: How do you feel when I mention him to you?

V: It feels pure and innocent.

C: So, there were no hurt feelings?

V: I just had a big vision. I left everything behind just to pursue this big vision, which I am currently working on.

C: Do you know where this vision is leading you?

V: When you have a plan, you just go for it. That's what I did to get a king. I think I just had this vision. Nothing could stop me, and it feels right to do so. I don't feel guilty...

It feels right; it feels like I was supposed to do that.

Then I was moved to the last day of that life, and I was asked to describe what I saw. All I could see were white clouds all around, nothing else. Often, people go through the experience of death, but for some reason, I chose to skip that part. Later on, I understood that I saw my death experience in the previous regression I described before. There was no need to see it again.

C: Can you feel your body?

V: No.

C: Are you outside of the body?

V: I think so.

C: How did you leave the body?

V: As I always do.

C: Did you die?

V: Yes. The vehicle is no longer needed. I am done.

C: How did it end?

V: I just exited...I left my body on Earth. I see pure light now.

C: How does it feel?

V: Home, finally.

Then Charbel replied that there is a lesson and a purpose to every existence. What lessons did that life teach you, and why did you have to live it?

V: When you set something in your mind, you just go for it.

No obstacles can stop you; just have the vision and follow every step to achieve it.

Go for it. Don't look to the sides; there are always obstacles and distractions. Go forward.

When you set the goal, hold it in your mind and don't get distracted or demotivated. If something is not going the way you want it to go, eventually you're going to go and get it.

C: What is the purpose of that lifetime?

V: To experience power and influence and to create a history that will be admired and cherished for many years to come.

Deep Conversation with the Subconscious

Moving forward, Charbel will engage in direct dialogue with the subconscious or SC (referred to as "they"– the collective energy). To proceed to the final stage of the session, he began addressing my questions from the list I brought with me. He was also curious why they were highlighting that one specific life among all the others and what kind of hidden secrets and meanings were waiting to be uncovered in the details of that past.

SC: Because she needed to see that when she doesn't belong to a certain level or community, she can still manage to be a part of it. Even if she thinks she doesn't belong. She came from being a normal woman and became a part of the court. She became one of the most important people and part of a group that you might think she doesn't belong to, but she made herself a part of it by working hard. In this life, she refuses to climb higher up the ladder because she is afraid of becoming famous and has some fears, but that life is a great example that showing that from nowhere, she can go somewhere, be somewhere, and create history.

C: But what is causing her fear?

SC: That people are going to judge her. Judgment.

C: How are you going to help her?

SC: She is writing a book right now. She is clearing a lot of her issues by writing, and she is also realizing that when she's writing, she is recalling her past memories and the lives that she's really proud of, that she was powerful. So she's basically collecting all those pieces, piece by piece, getting herself together into one piece. All her past lives—that's who she is today—are basically like she's collecting one missing piece after another and creating her own entity in this life.

C: Since you mentioned she is writing her book, what else can she write about other than the things she is writing about now?

SC: The first book is based on her own experiences. It's going to be more like an autobiography about her past lives and also her experiences during the guided meditations or Akashic records where she found out about her past or other parts of herself. But there are going to be more books to follow. She already has an idea she loves, but the first book is mainly about her own experiences.

C: So, is she on the right path with this project?

SC: Yes.

C: And why are all those challenges facing her?

SC: To make her stronger and see if she truly wants to do this, she should hold on to it or give up and say it's maybe not something for her.

C: What about the financial struggle?

SC: She needs to set priorities, determining what is most important for her at that moment. As soon as she sets all the priorities, everything is going to fall in the right direction. What is most important for her? She is asking for help, and she wants a shortcut; she wants the answers right away, but we want her to go inside and think for herself. She is creating her path.

C: Are there any money blocks?

SC: Not really; she has already worked on them. There are just a few obstacles in her way.

C: Obstacles like what?

SC: Money. Lack of money.

C: How is she going to solve this?

SC: She needs to learn how to set intentions and priorities, focusing on what is most important. Money can be a great distraction for everyone because a lack of money can divert you from your life purpose.

C: True.

SC: And if you feel weak, think, "Maybe this isn't for me." You might consider finding a side hustle to help you survive. What is the purpose of your life? What is your life's goal? What do you want to achieve? Therefore, you may need to step outside your comfort zone and find a side hustle for a few hours or days to overcome those obstacles. Some people are willing to take risks and focus on their main goal. For example, she is determined to continue pursuing her passion for writing a book. She believes that distractions are inevitable, but she perseveres and continues writing regardless.

C: How are you going to help her make an income?

SC: There is money coming. There might be a time when it's going to be tough, but it's not for a long time. Once she moves to Mount Shasta, she is going to do quantum healing hypnosis from Mount Shasta while working on her book.

C: So, you want her to move to Mount Shasta?

SC: Yes. Yes, and she agreed to it. It's not forever, but she needs to spend some time there. Consider it a continuing education in her life. She needs to be closer to the Masters. She needs to spend more time alone, meditating. She is going to receive messages, which she will share in her books, but we need her there physically.

C: How are you going to help her find the right apartment and the money to move?

SC: Exactly the way she has moved from the East Coast to the West Coast with $200 in her pocket. And here we go; she made it. We are always helping her. The right people and the right circumstances are always going to make themselves present.

C: Can you do a body scan?

SC: Yes, she is complaining about her vision.

C: True, what can you do about that?

SC: She is refusing to see some things for what they are, but we're showing her something she's refusing to accept. That's why she is losing her vision.

C: Things like what?

SC: That she is powerful. She has a God inside of her. She is the universe. She became a little more open to this concept through her clients, but there is still a little resistance. Once she accepts that she has power, she can create rain, and she can stop the rain. She has already done that. She changed the path of the hurricane so it didn't hit Miami when she was there. She did it; it was her job. Just face it and see it for what it is.

C: Are you going to heal her vision today?

SC: We can improve it a little bit.

C: Why not all?

SC: She needs to do her homework.

C: So you can clear it for her, and after this session, she will continue with her homework. You know vision is very important, especially for someone who is writing and spending a lot of time in front of a computer.

SC: Yeah.

As I paused to catch my breath, I felt the air filling my lungs deeply, almost like I was inhaling pure vitality. Charbel began to move on to the next question, but the subconscious urged him to wait just a moment longer until the healing process was complete.

C: What about her dizziness?

SC: She is getting a lot of downloads. It's okay. It's going to settle. She has been prepared for the next level, so...stay grounded. That's something she needs to go through to reach the next level. Her body, her physical body, is also expanding to accept bigger downloads, and there are more significant downloads coming, step by step. Sometimes she's stressed out and doing all the earthly stuff that keeps her out of balance. When she gets her next download, it's kind of too much for her. That's when she feels dizzy. However, when she keeps herself grounded, she doesn't feel dizzy but still receives the downloads. Just stay grounded and be aware of the energies she is receiving.

Continuing with the body scan, a few issues were detected and cleared.

SC: Her neck.

C: What is causing her neck to be stiff?

SC: Her posture. She is not using the right posture to read and write and has been sitting for hours.

C: Will you fix it for her today?

SC: Yeah, we can remove that buildup and adjust a little bit. (At that point, I turned my head to the sides and up and down.) She needs to stretch more. She is not sleeping on a good pillow. She has a better one. I am sending light to soothe her neck, but first, she needs to replace that pillow. That will make her feel a lot better.

C: Thank you. What else?

SC: Feet, not feeling the ground underneath, she is like flying and not finding the right place in her life. Also, she needs to walk barefoot at times, as the shoes she was wearing were not right for her. It's good that she threw away the slippers. They were not right for her, either. By walking with just her socks on or barefoot, she will notice an improvement.

C: Can you fix this issue as well?

SC: The improvement will come with time. We can alleviate cramps. She needs to use the massage ball with needles she has at home and just put it under her sole. There are some spots she needs to activate on her feet. It's also going to improve her vision. She can do it on her own. She has some massage tools. Right now, I'm touching that spot with a big toe—that spot she needs to work on. It's going to improve her foot health; her headaches are going to go away; and it will also improve her vision.

I could feel the pain from a toe pressing into my sole; they were showing me the spot.

C: What about her hormone levels and diet?

SC: Hormones are fine. Her diet is good. It is great that she removed meat from her diet. We are proud of her for that. She might want to include some juices and smoothies for added vitamins.

There was a little bit of unhealthy bacteria in her stomach; it came from the water. The water in her apartment building is not good. But once she moves, it is going to improve by itself. We already told her to drink only spring water on Mount Shasta and not to consume bottled water at all. The tap water on Mount Shasta is healthy. However, the tap water in her apartment building is not good at all, and even the filter doesn't help. She is buying bottled water to drink, which is fine, but she still uses tap water for cooking. This is creating bad bacteria in her stomach.

C: What about her chakras? Are they balanced?

SC: The root chakra is a little bit out of balance.

C: Can you balance it for her?

SC: Yes...her heart chakra is also.

C: Can you work on that as well?

SC: She needs to watch her thoughts and her feelings. She has been managing well lately; she became more aware of her emotions and thoughts and started to control them. But once something happens, like bad news, they still throw her off her feet. She needs to find the balance to get back into her element and not allow bad energy to take over for too long. This is for everybody as well. Bad emotions, fear, and stress are all low-vibration energy. You lose connection with the source when you allow those negativities to take over. To restore the connection, you need to keep your balance and find your inner core to connect again. And when you feel connected you won't panic.

Her ears. That part is a little bit blocked (I was showing which part). That's because she allowed herself to hear what she was not supposed to hear, like negativity and being around negative influences. That's why she feels pressure in her ears. Just accept it and let go; it's in the past. Allow yourself to make mistakes and let them go. What's done is done. Also, there is some fogginess in her brain.

C: Are you going to remove that?

SC: Yes...it comes from her thoughts that are causing the fog. We are removing it as if with a vacuum, sucking it out. She is going to have more clarity.

C: Are there any energy blocks?

SC: Yes, her knees. She is refusing to walk forward.

C: Can you clarify that?

SC: Yes, but she needs to work on that as well. She needs to remove the fear that she might be punished for spreading out the information that she signed up for before she came here. Eventually, she will need to cross that river of fear and insecurity, align with herself, and fulfill her mission and her life purpose.

C: Why did she feel the vibration in her body and the feeling of nausea?

SC: She experienced stress and received downloads. When she is stressed and receives a lot of new energy without alignment, it causes her to feel like vomiting. As we mentioned before, she needs to maintain a high vibration and stay in alignment. More downloads will continue to come. When she is stressed, she is out of alignment, and the downloads still need to occur. If she allows herself to become stressed, she will not be able to handle it.

C: What are all those issues with her apartment? What is this for?

SC: If she were comfortable there, she would renew the lease and stay. The same goes for the clients: if she had a lot of clients, she would be busy at this location, but she needs to move. It might take her until summertime when her lease expires, but she is not going to even think about renewing it. She will be happy to be out of there.

C: But why do you want her to move to that area? What is special about it that is not here?

SC: Mount Shasta. She knows about it. There is Telos underneath Mount Shasta. She's aware of it. Adama has contacted her as well. Mount Shasta is calling people. You need to receive a call to move there. She can call you, and she can also kick you out of there. She can make your life miserable, and you have no choice but to move away. But she is going to call certain people at a certain time for future education, evolution, and a learning experience. And she needs this learning experience to better do her job on Earth. This is when we are approaching the deadline for her to do that. And she has accepted the call. She is not going to be there forever, just for a certain period of time. We cannot say how many months or years; when she is done, she's going to know she's done.

C: Is there any connection between her and Adama?

SC: Yes, he is her teacher. She's going to be working closely with him.

C: So, that's why she was called to go to Mount Shasta?

SC: Yes...Saint Germain will also be present. He will teach her many things during her time there. She will have the opportunity to see him in physical form. Additionally, she will meet people who are not widely known. To truly learn about and connect with them, she must be present in that community. These individuals are incredibly valuable and important in her life, playing a crucial role in her next steps and personal evolution.

C: Why is she receiving all that information about Saint Germain?

SC: Because he is her master. He is preparing her to impart the information he knows, which she can then share on Earth while she has a physical body. Together, they are going to write a book. Saint Germain, an Ascended Master, will guide her as she uses her body to write and share knowledge with people. And he has been preparing her for years in different incarnations.

Even if it was for a short period, there was an activation made that now, once she's going to meet him, she's going to be prepared. Also, her physical body is adjusting to the energies that she can handle.

C: What is her mission exactly? Is she on the right path with her mission?

SC: Yes.

C: Could you tell her more about it?

SC: Her mission is to expand consciousness on Earth. She is aware of it, but she doesn't want to admit it. She is part of the awakening process. While she doesn't believe she has the power to assist people in their awakening journey, she does possess that ability.

And that life as Madame de Pompadour, Elizabeth...we showed Elizabeth because Elizabeth yelled at people that she had power, and now Volha says that she doesn't have power. Who am I to do that? We want her to know that she used to have that power. She had a great influence and people are still writing and talking about her. She has already had other incarnations, but people are still talking about her previous incarnations. She does have power, and she has the power now to help humanity expand consciousness on the planet.

C: So, was she Elizabeth in her past life, or was it just an imprint?

SC: It was her life, her father was Robert (Robert Dudley). Yes, she got it right.

C: What can you tell her about that past life?

SC: She had great power; she led wars, managed people, and created history as a woman. And now she is a woman, and she cannot even open her mouth.

C: Why did she have to incarnate with her father?

SC: To learn the lesson...and her mother.

C: What is the lesson behind it?

SC: The lesson is to love each other. They are a family, so they have to love each other. There is no choice. They have to learn to love each other...and her mother as well.

C: Was her father Robert Dudley?

SC: Yes.

C: And what about her mom?

SC: Amy...Robert's wife...who had an accident. It was not an accident. She was standing in the way between two lovers, and they got rid of her. That's why she feels heaviness. She feels guilt. That guilt has been following her for years and many incarnations. And that she doesn't get along with her mother as well. She needs to learn to forgive, ask for forgiveness, and learn to love and accept her mother as her mother in this life...you agreed to it!

C: Could you tell her about the relationship between Elizabeth and Francis Bacon?

SC: Yeah, that's her son.

C: He was her son?!

SC: Yes.

C: Was she a part of his life?

SC: Partially. She was so afraid to get her mother's feelings involved that she acted very cold. But on the side, she was following his life, yes.

C: What could you tell her about Elizabeth's life that has an impact on her life now?

SC: Lonely. The lonely life of a powerful woman who could have created a loving relationship, had a child, built a family, lost everything, and simply been a woman. She could have experienced the feelings of being a woman, a lover, and a mother, but she refused to embrace them. Instead, she pushed them away, becoming cold like a robot, suppressing all emotions.

C: But why is a woman like Elizabeth so powerful, but in this life, she's not the same? She doesn't have the same power.

SC: Remember karma: you want to be powerful, and you want to experience what it means to not have the power to even karma. In one life, you want to be wealthy, and in another, you want to be a beggar. You want to experience every side. You want to experience feelings and emotions from everybody on each side. So in that life, she was powerful, but in this life, she is not powerful yet. She has the potential to be, but she needs to work towards it. She must awaken the power within, tap into the memory of that power, a memory of strength, and move forward. She questions why Elizabeth would choose to incarnate in a village somewhere in Eastern Europe. It is to follow a path, evolve, experience, grow, and believe in her power. She needs to realize that whatever she dreams of, she can achieve it, but she must first be born into a poor family. She chose to be in that family, knowing that she wanted to see the other side of the coin.

C: You know that she has doubts about her past life. Why is this so? How can we give her more proof?

SC: She is going to make more discoveries about her past that will confirm it. For example, she recently received information about her father out of nowhere, which took her by surprise. She even asked us to stop revealing details because it felt awkward. She had dreams of being intimate with her father when she was in her 20s, and it turned out to be a recall from her past life. At that time, she wasn't aware of it, but once she learned about her past life as Elizabeth and her relationship with Robert, the dream started to make sense. It wasn't just a dream; it was a memory from the past life that now makes sense. There are more things she will understand later that will start to make sense, and all the pieces of the puzzle will come together. Saint Germain is helping her by presenting all those books to read for confirmation because he knows. He is part of this game as well...Saint Germain was a big part of her life during King Louis XV's time. They had a connection in that past life too.

C: Does she have any other historical past lives that she needs to know about?

SC: Not that she needs to know at this particular time. We cannot provide her with any additional information, as she needs time to digest the information she already has.

C: Did you give her too much information to digest?

SC: Those two lives are enough for now.

C: Why is she still single?

SC: She needs to finish some projects because she knows who he is, and he is very handsome. She would throw everything away just to be with him and would not follow her path. So we want her to do her project first, and as a final surprise, she's going to get him...as the cherry on the pie, not the cherry first. She needs to get the pie first and then comes the cherry. She has projects to do without him – alone. He's there; he is not going anywhere, but she needs to do her homework.

C: Can you give me a time frame?

SC: Around six months, up to a year.

C: You promised...you promised it before, and it didn't happen.

SC: Well, we didn't promise her anything; we just informed her. However, we don't have a specific time frame. The timing will depend on when her current project is completed and she can move on to the next one. If she remains stuck on the current project for years, she will only meet him after that. If she continues working on her project as planned, the meeting could happen within a few months to a year. It's not as simple as saying she will meet him in six months and then take a vacation to Hawaii during that time. That would not be beneficial and would postpone the meeting. It's not about the time; it's about how you use the time. What are you doing with the time that is bringing you closer to him?

C: Does she have a home planet?

SC: Yes...Electra. A purple planet.

I Am Electra, One of the Seven Sisters

A few years ago, as I was taking my dog for an early morning walk, a thunderous inner voice resonated in my mind, declaring, "I am Electra, one of the seven sisters." Instantly, an energetic surge seemed to spring from my chest and solar plexus area, triggering a wave of goosebumps across my entire body, causing me to spin around in awe. It was an incredible, potent experience. It felt as though some dormant part of me had been activated. Every time I affirmed, "I am Electra," it seemed to trigger this energy activation, enveloping my entire physical form.

The same sensation rippled through me each time I affirmed this newfound identity as if I was both the caller and recipient of a cosmic message. I was in awe of the transformation taking place within me as if I had connected with an ancient force—a lineage lying dormant in my soul for countless generations.

My curiosity led me to research the Pleiades, the seven sisters, and specifically Electra. In Greek mythology, Electra was the offspring of Atlas, doomed to hold up the world, and the nymph Pleione. I was beginning to grasp that this was more than a spiritual awakening; it was as if a part of my soul, long buried, was being unearthed. I felt a deep connection to the cosmos, a sense of belonging that surpassed the material world.

My bond with Electra deepened. My intuition was sharper, my dreams became more lucid and prophetic, and my senses seemed to harmonize with the world around me. By embracing my bond with Electra, I had awakened a part of myself that was ancient, potent, and deeply connected to the cosmos. It was a journey of self-discovery, self-empowerment, and spiritual awakening.

I never thought I could be from that planet. Yet the birthmarks on my right arm, forming the shape of the seven sisters, provided a profound insight. The birthmarks were not just peculiar skin pigments but a constellation, a sign of my celestial lineage. They were my guide, my compass pointing towards home—a home I never knew I had but somehow always longed for.

C: What are the characteristics of that planet? Can you tell me?

SC: It is similar to fairies and fairy tales—something magical, surreal, almost childish.

C: So...it's a beautiful planet?

SC: Yes, but she wanted to have an experience with all the negativities and emotions, so she's experiencing them now.

C: So...there are no negatives and no emotions?

SC: They are always happy; they're playing. Sometimes it is boring...they're always happy and all the same.

C: So, do you mean the emotions are for entertainment?

SC: Like stress and fear, we don't have it, but she wanted to experience it. She's getting it now.

C: What is the purpose of experiencing all those emotions?

SC: This is for soul evolution. You have different incarnations, and in each incarnation, you experience different emotions. They are also important for your soul and its history, essentially collecting various experiences from different incarnations.

C: When does the soul graduate?

SC: Never – You are always expanding. There is infinity. You can reach higher levels, but there is always room to grow. As you grow, you also teach.

C: Why do they (spirit guides) call her 'darling'?

SC: Saint Germain calls her 'darling'. He had also spent a lot of time in Europe. It comes from the British.

C: Does she have to move this mid-March or stay longer to finish what she has started?

SC: Keep working on the book. Forget about it for now.

C: So, she doesn't have to move in the middle of March?

SC: Not yet. We will inform her of the exact date later. However, she should start preparing for the move. It is likely to happen between mid-March and summer, but not immediately.

C: How did Elizabeth feel about giving her son away?

SC: Horrible, she suppressed all her emotions and became a very cold, emotionless lady. But deep inside, she was regretting and blaming herself for pushing away all the motherly feelings. She screamed and yelled a lot just to kill that feeling.

C: Are they preparing her for her ascension?

SC: If she wants to...she has done a lot, and she has evolved a lot. If she wants to, she can ask us, and we will guide her, but we know that she doesn't want it. She wants to keep working on the planet, on Earth, and she wants to have a baby. She wants to experience it. She wants to balance her karma. She wants to give birth to a baby. She wants to create a loving relationship to experience what it feels like to have a husband and a child, and she has a right to do that. She doesn't have to ascend. She can keep going and just balance her karma; what Elizabeth could not create, she can create now in this life.

C: What is her relationship to Jesus?

SC: She will come to it later, but they do have a connection.

C: Is there anything she needs to know about Sharula Dux?

SC: It was her on Mount Shasta...she's going to be around. She (Volha) can reach out to her anytime she needs help; she's going to hear her and help her, and once Volha is in Mount Shasta and needs help, she can reach out to Sharula for guidance to connect her with people who can help locally.

I was prompted to ask about her after a recent telepathic encounter where a voice introduced herself as Sharula Dux, a Princess of Telos, during one of my meditations. Her presence intrigued me, and I wanted to know why she had come. She reminded me of a prior agreement with my spirit guides to notify me when it was time to move. After confirming my recollection, she said that she was here to deliver a warning that the time for action was drawing near.

I typically receive guidance from my spiritual guides as a heads-up when it's time for me to relocate, allowing me to prepare, pack my belongings, and plan for the transition. Sometimes, the exact timing of the move is uncertain. However, these moves usually signify a shift to a new location for a specific purpose, such as embarking on a new project, learning something new, or fulfilling a commitment that I made before coming to Earth.

C: How is she evolving on her path since she started practicing quantum healing hypnosis?

SC: Greatly, we are proud of her. Her consciousness is expanding and will continue to evolve, with the next step on the horizon.

C: You know that she has an ex-lover?

SC: Yes.

C: How is he affecting her life?

SC: He is draining her energy.

C: How can she stop that?

SC: Stop communicating; cut the cord.

C: Just like that, so easy?

SC: Yes. Don't answer his messages; just ignore him.

C: Is it going to be easy for her to do so?

SC: No, he's kind of the stronger one, but he has a mission to distract her from her purpose. Sometimes he does it well, and sometimes not. Occasionally, he shakes her, making her feel unsteady on the ground. He is also teaching her a lesson on being grounded and cautious about where her energy goes—her communications, her surroundings—so she does not lose her energy and then asks for our help. When she stops giving away her energy to people who are unnecessary and do not help her in her life, she will have more energy for herself and her projects, and she will ask for help less often. Of course, we are helping her, but she also needs to be aware of where her energy and focus are directed.

C: How is she going to feel after the healing process is complete?

SC: Lighter. Much lighter.

C: Does everything look okay?

SC: Yes. She needed this reset to clear any obstacles from her path. We want her to just keep going forward without looking to the sides or behind. The most important thing is what is now and in front of her; everything else is not important.

C: Do you have any last messages for her?

SC: Keep going. Don't stop...we are always supporting you. We are always here to help, even turning the impossible into possible. Even if it's not your turn to receive something, we can manipulate digital numbers and make it your turn now if necessary. We can manipulate time, shift realities, and do whatever it takes for you. But if it's not meant to be, we will do everything to prevent it and you need just to accept it. If we are blocking something for you, trust that there is a reason behind it. Some things may not make sense now, but they will become clear later... just trust.

The session was intense yet enlightening. I gained a deep understanding of the life of Elizabeth I, her resilience, and her fears. I discovered the power she held, the sacrifices she made, the challenges she faced, and the loneliness she endured. I learned about her strength, her wisdom, and her unwavering dedication to her kingdom.

These insights not only quenched my curiosity but further assisted me in recognizing my advantages and disadvantages. The session gave me a fresh perspective and a new lens through which to view my current life. It made me realize that I was much stronger than I believed and that the trials and tribulations I currently face are just a part of my journey, just like they were for Elizabeth I.

As I emerged from the hypnosis, I felt a deep connection to Elizabeth I and Madame de Pompadour, two powerful women who left a lasting impact on history during the

16th and 18th centuries, respectively. Both women have defied societal expectations and wielded power in their respective spheres, leaving a lasting impact on the history of their countries and the world. Their legacies as strong, independent women who navigated the complexities of politics, power, and influence continue to inspire and captivate people to this day.

The session ended, leaving me with a sense of peace and clarity. It was as though a weight had been taken off my shoulders. It was a unique and enlightening experience, one that I will cherish for the rest of my life.

This experience was a powerful reminder that it's essential to trust the process and allow the subconscious to guide us. It's not about fulfilling our fantasies or curiosities, but about understanding our past lives in a way that can help us grow and evolve in our current lives. I felt humbled and grateful for this enlightening journey, and I was ready to share this insight with the world.

19

Symbolic Dream: Key to My Soul

The dream I had the other night was truly extraordinary. In the ethereal world of my slumber, I found myself transported to the familiar setting of my grandmother's old bedroom. Though she has long since passed away, I have always felt a deep connection with her that transcends the boundaries of life and death.

As I stood in the room, I was immediately drawn to her bed, where an array of keys of varying shapes and sizes were strewn about, mingling with a heart-shaped hanger. It was as if a mysterious puzzle awaited my deciphering.

At that moment, the realization dawned on me that uncovering the matching key would be no simple feat. The task seemed daunting, as though it would require an eternity to find the one that fits just right. Yet, almost as soon as I embarked on my quest, my eyes fell upon the perfect key. It was as if it had been waiting for me all along, a key that held the power to unlock something profound within me—my very heart, the deepest secrets of my soul. The sense of discovery and connection that washed over me was nothing short of transformative. It felt like my grandma gave me a confirmation of my self-discovery and that I was on the right path.

This dream experience reaffirmed my belief in the interconnectedness of all beings, not just within the tangible realm of our existence but also across the vast expanses of time and space.

We are all interwoven in the grand tapestry of life, our threads crossing and intersecting, creating a beautiful pattern of relationships, experiences, and lessons. This realization is not just about my personal journey but serves as a reminder that we are all part of a larger, universal narrative. Our lives, our stories, are not merely our own but are interconnected with those of every soul we come across.

This energy is not confined by the constraints of time or space. It is eternally flowing, eternally evolving, connecting us all in an intricate dance of life and death, joy and sorrow, creation and destruction. We are one

Acknowledgements

I want to sincerely thank my family and friends for their continuous support and encouragement during this life-changing experience. Your love and belief in me have been a source of strength and inspiration. To my mentors and spiritual teachers, thank you for guiding me with wisdom and compassion and for sharing your profound knowledge and insights that have enriched my spiritual growth. Special acknowledgment goes to Jeff Bennett and Charbel Nader for their invaluable Quantum Healing Hypnosis sessions.

A heartfelt thank you to my loyal companion, Kiki, whose unconditional love and presence brought joy and comfort during the writing of this book.

I am immensely grateful to my spiritual guides—Adama, Archangel Michael, my Pleiadian star family, Saint Germain, and Dolores Cannon—for their divine guidance, protection, and illuminating presence throughout this sacred exploration of past lives and reincarnation.

Your wisdom, love, and support have been a guiding light on this profound journey of self-discovery and spiritual awakening.

With deep appreciation,
Volha Zhamoitsina

Born in 1982 in Belarus, a small country in Eastern Europe, Volha Zhamoitsina's passion for creativity and design started to blossom early on. She followed her love for fashion to Hamburg, Germany, after finishing high school, where she enrolled at the Hamburg University of Applied Sciences to pursue her dream of becoming a fashion designer. Immersing herself in the world of fashion, she took every opportunity to gain industry experience and even had the chance to travel to Paris for fashion week, further fueling her passion for the industry.

After graduating, Volha made a big move to Los Angeles to explore different career paths in the movie industry and real estate. However, it wasn't until she found herself on the West Coast of Florida that she discovered her true calling in hypnotherapy and past life regression. Through training and certification, she became a certified hypnotherapist, past life regression specialist, and Quantum Healing Hypnosis practitioner.

Returning to Los Angeles with her new skills and passion for helping others, Volha now focuses on guiding individuals toward personal growth and self-healing through hypnotherapy, quantum healing hypnosis, and past life regression. Known for her compassionate approach and dedication to assisting others on their journey to self-discovery, Volha Zhamoitsina continues to make a positive impact in the lives of those she works with.

www.hypnovz.com

Books By This Author

FROM MT. SHASTA WITH LOVE

Listening to the Sacred Whisper of the Mountain

Have you ever felt a mysterious calling from a sacred place — as if a mountain, a forest, or the Earth itself was trying to speak to you? Do you sense that there is more to this world than meets the eye — hidden realms, inner worlds, and ancient beings who guide us when we dare to listen?

In *From Mt. Shasta with Love*, Volha Zhamoitsina shares her extraordinary journey into the mystical heart of Mount Shasta. Through vivid personal experiences, Inner-Earth travels, and direct conversations with the consciousness of the mountain itself, she reveals how these profound encounters have shaped her own awakening and deepened her connection to Source.

In *From Mt. Shasta with Love*, you'll discover:

- How a sacred mountain can serve as a portal to higher dimensions and Inner-Earth civilizations.
- The hidden wisdom that comes from listening deeply to nature and honoring the living consciousness of the Earth.

- Personal revelations and spiritual insights drawn from past life connections, multidimensional awareness, and soul memories.
- How awakening is not a destination, but a continual unfolding through trust, surrender, and love.
- Word-for-word dialogues from several remarkable regression sessions.

And so much more...

Index

1. Adama, High Priest of Telos, the Light city underneath Mt. Shasta, CA.

2. Amy Robsart (1532–1560), first wife of Robert Dudley.

3. Aurelia Louise Jones Telos, Volume 2: Messages for the Enlightenment of a Humanity in Transformation, Mount Shasta Light Publishing Copyright 2004, p. 80.

4. Aurelia Louise Jones Telos, Volume 3: Protocols of the Fifth Dimension, Mount Shasta Light Publishing, Copyright 2006, p. 42, p. 72–73.

5. Claire Heartsong and Catherine Ann Clementt, Understanding Twin Flame Union: the Ascension of St. Germain and Portia, S.E.E. Publishing, Copyright 2011, p. 86, p. 100.

6. Dolores Cannon (1931–2014) was an American author and hypnotherapist.

7. Dolores Cannon, The Keepers of the Garden, Ozark Mountain Publishing, Copyright 1993, p. 70.

8. Francis Bacon (1561–1626), English Renaissance philosopher.

9. King of France, Louis XV (1710–1774).

10. Madame de Pompadour (1721–1764) was the mistress of King Louis XV and a member of the French court.

11. Queen Elizabeth I (1533–1603), Queen of England and daughter of Henry VIII.

12.   Robert Dudley (1532–1588), 1st Earl of Leicester, was an English statesman.

13.   Sharula Dux (1725- current), Princess of Telos.